Praise for *Let's Play*

"*Let Them Play* showed us how to defend play. Jeff and Denita's second book, *Let's Play*, shows us *how to* play. It is by far the best and most original book of ideas for any early childhood learning environment. I highly recommend it to anyone who works with or cares for young children in any setting, be that a child care center, a family child care home, a preschool environment, or a parent!"

> —Tracy Hinton, family child care provider

"If you wonder what play-based education looks like, this is it. This book makes you rethink your approach to education and will inspire you throughout your day, month, and year. It's a great read with the right amount of fun, and the sentence 'A chainsaw would be overkill' alone will make you laugh out loud. More importantly, this book has made me a better teacher and has given me the research-based confidence to make play the centerpiece of the classroom. I wish someone had put this book into my hands on my first day on the job."

> —Peggie Bobo, lead teacher at All Saints School and partner/founder of Small Kids. Big Ideas.

"Thank you to Jeff and Denita for writing another meaningful book for lovers of all things play. This one picks up where *Let Them Play* left off. Full of inspiring ideas, utilizing easy-to-find, yet un-conventional, materials, it will surely spark your imagination. I sent my husband to Home Depot with my first shopping list before I had even finished chapter one!"

> —Michelle Lewis-Barnes, owner of Busy Bee Preschool

"Jeff A. Johnson and Denita Dinger have BIG, messy, imaginative ideas that young children will love and learn from. As a music teacher, I'm especially excited to try the Packing Tape Drum and Not a Rain Stick, but all the adventures are amazing and, best of all, completely play-based. If young children could design their own '(un)curriculum,' it would look a lot like *Let's Play*."

> —Abigail Flesch Connors, author of *101 Rhythm Instrument Activities for Young Children*

"*Let's Play* is full of fantastic inspiration for play and sure to spur the imagination of adults and children alike! Filled with possibilities (and variations) for exciting, hands-on play activities, you can pull it out when you need some inspiration, or use it to plan ahead for a more challenging play-filled project to embark on together. Rich with ideas for exploration, this is a must-have resource for anyone looking to enjoy the excitement of playing and learning together with young children. Now, come on—*Let's Play*!"

> —Molly Hughes, family child care provider

"No matter where you are on your journey toward promoting play in early childhood, you will find invaluable ideas inside the pages of this book—from messy to non-messy, from simple to complex, from music to science to literacy, and more. Jeff and Denita have included a treasure trove of ideas to challenge and intrigue children and adults alike. This is a must-have for bookshelves (and, more importantly, in the hands) of parents, caregivers, and teachers of young children."

—Stacey Feehan, preschool teacher, mom, and promoter of play

"As a speech language pathologist working with multicultural children—children with learning disabilities, in particular—I know that play-based therapy engages children. It can be the best way to observe children's sensory, motor, and cognitive abilities. *Let's Play* explains the rich complexity of spontaneous play and its opportunities for learning and rehabilitation."

—Paola Orlando, speech language pathologist

"I was scanning the table of contents, and when I got to chapter twenty, I said to myself, 'This is going to be an incredible book of fun.' I was right! Thirty-nine chapters of 'bodies and brains engaged' play experiences and oozing over with fun! Reflective, intentional teachers, those who like to fly by the seat of their pants, and every teaching style in between will find something wonderful to experience with children in *Let's Play*. The book list at the end of each chapter is a bonus!"

—Joyce Mahl, child care consultant

"*Let's Play* is just the advocate child-led learning has been waiting for. The fresh, open-ended ideas are presented with wit and encouragement and are manageable enough that anyone can implement them into play time with children."

—Denise Milley, special education developmental teacher

"I've been anticipating this book ever since reading *Let Them Play*. I've been gradually shifting to an open-ended play-based experience for my group, so I love the ideas presented in this book. They are inexpensive, easy to gather, and mostly readily available. I also like that each idea tied into what the children were learning. There were a few ideas—worms—that would push my comfort zone, but I know they're all activities the children will LOVE!"

—Shannon Grant, family child care provider

Let's Play

Also by Jeff A. Johnson and Denita Dinger

Let Them Play:

An Early Learning (Un)Curriculum

Let's Play

(Un)Curriculum Early Learning Adventures

Jeff A. Johnson and Denita Dinger

Redleaf Press®
www.redleafpress.org
800-423-8309

Published by Redleaf Press
10 Yorkton Court
St. Paul, MN 55117
www.redleafpress.org

First edition 2014
Cover design by Jim Handrigan
Cover photograph by Heather Jones
Interior design by Hillspring Books, Inc.
Typeset in Myriad Pro
Interior photographs by Jeff A. Johnson and Denita Dinger, except photographs on pages xvi, 91, 93, and 94 by Sandra Cole; photographs on pages 54 and 55 by Tammy Lockwood; and photographs on pages 79, 80, 160, and 161 by Lisa Ditlefsen
Printed in the United States of America

21 20 19 18 17 16 15 14   1 2 3 4 5 6 7 8

Library of Congress Cataloging-in-Publication Data
Johnson, Jeff A., 1969-
  Let's play : (un)curriculum early learning adventures / Jeff A. Johnson, Denita Dinger.
     pages cm
  Summary: "Let's Play provides a variety of budget-friendly, child-centered experiences that lead to countless learning opportunities. Each chapter outlines an open-ended play adventure with instructions, photographs, and fresh ideas for children to explore everything from worms to magnets" — Provided by publisher.
  ISBN 978-1-60554-127-3 (pbk.)
  ISBN 978-1-60554-342-0 (e-book)
  1. Play—United States. 2. Early childhood education—United States. 3. Early childhood education—Curricula—United States. 4. Early childhood education—Activity programs—United States. I. Dinger, Denita. II. Title.
  LB1139.35.P55J66 2014
  372.21—dc23
                        2013032806

Printed on acid-free paper

To my family—my trusting parents, who let me use my imagination and learn in a way that gifted me with magical childhood memories; my son, who is always solving and wondering and is determined to find a better way to do almost everything; my daughter, who shines a unique light on almost every situation and has an unfailing imagination; my husband, who has been my pillar through countless journeys and believes in me, even when he knows better

—Denita

To Rowan Lenore—keep playing, little Bunny

—Jeff

Contents

Acknowledgments

We would both like to acknowledge everyone at Redleaf Press who made it possible for you to read this book.

Thanks also to Beth Wallace for once again using her keen editor's eye to mold our ideas into a readable and useful format.

Thanks to Maryann Harman (musicwithmar.com) for help with selecting songs to share.

Thanks to Alec Duncan for sharing the activities in chapters 14 and 15.

Thanks to all the early learning professionals who helped test-drive these projects: Angie Vinson, Bill Buss, Brenda Harms, Brenda Novack, Emily Plank, Erica Kimmel, Jen Johnstonbaugh, Jen Shaffer, Jennifer Smyth, JoAnn Steinly, Joanna Hatton, Lisa Ditlefsen, Maree Naera, Melinda Carlson, Melissa Lawwell, Sandra Cole, Susan Dotson, Tammy Kirk, Wanda Sowden.

Thanks to Erin Hammitt and everyone at St. Peter's Child Care in Jefferson, South Dakota, where we got to take some photos.

● ● ●

In appreciation of moments, all of which I am extremely thankful for. Moments that are filled with laughter and tears. Moments full of learning through succeeding as well as failing. Moments when my husband just nods as I blurt out new ideas that nonchalantly wander into my head. Moments that create sparkles in the eyes of my own children as well as my "littles." Moments that are full of opportunities and moments that make you pause and appreciate.

—Denita

Thanks to Tasha, my *One True Love*. Thanks for tolerating the messes that came with testing ideas for this book.

Thanks to Jitters Coffee and Donuts on Pearl Street in Sioux City, Iowa—your yummy Sunshine donuts and great staff (Sarah, Lori, Alexa, Amy, Melaine, and Magdalena) made the shop a cozy place to write.

Thanks to Starbucks 9602 and the twenty or so other Starbucks locations around the country that provided good chai and comfortable space for writing.

—Jeff

Introduction

Let's Play: (Un)Curriculum Early Learning Adventures is a follow-up to our 2012 book, *Let Them Play: An Early Learning (Un)Curriculum,* and is intended for early learning professionals and families who want to support hands-on, child-led, play-based learning. *Let's Play* offers up simple, engaging, and learning-rich play experiences for young children. It helps adults accustomed to rigidly structured, adult-led early learning curriculums ease into an (un)curriculum that supports good old-fashioned play and trusts kids as learners. Easing into an (un)curriculum is important, because for many people, the idea of giving up control and letting children lead learning is very scary.

Think of the following information as the book's FAQ page. If an (un)curriculum is new to you, the FAQs will bring you up to speed.

What is an (un)curriculum?

An (un)curriculum is hands-on, child-led, play-based learning supported by the preparation, encouragement, and facilitation of an adult. Here's some additional information about an (un)curriculum:

- *An (un)curriculum is supported by brain development research.*
  (Un)curriculums are built on research about what young brains need, how they work, and how they learn.

- *An (un)curriculum nurtures the individual child.*
  Good early learning is not so much about wooden blocks, toy trucks, baby dolls, fingerpaint, and picture books as it is about relationships. It's about the emotional environment as opposed to the physical environment. It's about

engaging individual children as unique people and then nurturing their needs, trusting them as learners, and supporting their growth.

- *An (un)curriculum sees everything as a learning opportunity.*
  In an (un)curriculum, the job of the caregiver is to see learning moments and make the most of them, building on the child's prior knowledge and life experience. Luckily, everything offers a chance to engage the world, make a connection, and gain understanding: a cardboard box, a disagreement with peers, a broken spiderweb near the front door.

- *An (un)curriculum is based on children's needs, likes, and interests.*
  In an (un)curriculum, great care is taken by the adult to ensure that all aspects of the program are geared toward supporting the unique needs of the individual children.

- *An (un)curriculum supports children's autonomy.*
  In an (un)curriculum, children are trusted as learners and as much as possible are given control over the four Ts: Team, Time, Task, and Technique.

- *An (un)curriculum focuses on children's play.*
  A commitment to play is the defining feature of an (un)curriculum.

What ages are the activities designed for?

The target age range for these activities is children age three to six years, but younger and older children will also enjoy and learn from most of the activities.

How does this book help me support play and learning?

This book helps you change your curriculum in several ways:

- It provides instructions for activities that are full of learning and really fun.
- It offers activity variations that will help keep the play going.
- It suggests books and songs that expand on ideas and interests related to the activity.
- It encourages the adult to reinterpret, reinvent, and reimagine our suggestions based on the interests of the children, the materials at hand, and his or her own imagination.
- It helps the adult learn to relax, to let go, and to trust in play.

How is this book structured?

Each chapter outlines a play adventure with an overview, a list of ingredients, step-by-step instructions, a variety of variations, and related books and songs the adult can use to keep the play-based learning going. We've left some space at the end of each chapter to jot down notes about how the kids respond to the activity, to scribble new ideas, and to keep track of what preparation and facilitation techniques work best. Each chapter ends with suggestions for choosing your next play adventure.

How should I use this book?

We hope you will use this book as the foundation for an (un)curriculum, but how you do that depends on your needs:

- You can ink activities from this book on your calendar for the next six months and then stick to our instructions when it comes time to play.
- You can pull activities from this book when they connect to something the children are interested in. For example, if one week the kids are particularly into blocks, you might want to do the Peanut Butter Jar Blocks adventure you'll find in chapter 7 (page 30).

- You can take this book off the shelf now and then use it when you have an empty spot to fill in your day.
- You can use this book to spark your own imagination and inspire fresh new play ideas.

Are these activities kid tested and caregiver approved?

They sure are. As we developed the activities, we tested them with the children in our own child care programs. Once we had projects we felt worked, we wrote them up and sent them out to a committed squad of Test Drivers for review. We then used their feedback to refine the projects. Once you've done the projects, we'd love to hear all about your ideas and experiences too. Visit our Facebook page, www.facebook.com/LetThemPlayBook, to share.

How involved should kids be in building and setting up projects?

As involved as they can be. In a properly supervised setting, kids can handle all the building or setup involved in these projects. For some adults, it may mean trusting kids a bit more than usual or going a bit outside their comfort zone, but it's worth the effort. Let kids own the whole process.

Is it really okay to let kids play with bricks, sticks, and other potentially dangerous items?

We think so—as long as the adult in the room is tuned in, attentive, and focused on creating an engaging but safe environment. You obviously can't hand a roomful of three-year-olds glue guns, wish them luck, and go watch Dr. Oz. You can, however, control your environment in such a way that kids can safely do some hot gluing.

For children to learn to assess and manage risk takes practice. Sometimes that practice comes with a pinched toe or a bumped head. The pinch and the bump are part of the learning process. If we try to avoid all the potential pinches and bumps, then we steal the learning opportunities that come with them, and we prevent kids from developing their confidence, knowledge of the world, self-awareness, and other beneficial skills.

Can I make changes to the adventures that will allow kids who have temperament or sensory issues to feel more comfortable with the projects?

Of course. These projects are just a starting point. We encourage you to customize them to meet the needs of the kids in your care. Knowing the kids well enough to understand their unique needs is an important part of any (un)curriculum. Sometimes a small change will be enough—offering a child who does not like noise a pair of ear plugs during loud play, or giving a long-handled spoon to a child with sensory issues so he can stir the glop other kids are elbow deep in. Other times, children may choose to opt out and watch from the sidelines. That should be okay too.

Is it okay to substitute materials when I don't agree with the suggested ones—food items that won't be consumed, for example?

Sure it is. We don't want you to do anything that you feel uncomfortable with. The projects were all designed for flexibility.

How should I introduce the activities to the kids?

Here are some of our favorite ways to get going:

- *Follow their lead.*
  Wait until the kids show an interest in a topic or an object that somehow relates to the activity, and then use that as an opening to introduce the activity.

- *Practice plopping.*

  We introduced the term *plop* in our book *Let Them Play*. When you *plop*, you simply put the activity ingredients out for the kids to discover and then step back and wait to see what happens. We use *plop* a lot throughout this book because it's our favorite way to share new play ideas with the children.

- *Hide the ingredients.*

  Think of this as clandestine plopping. Don't plop the materials or prompts out in the open. Instead, use your imagination and make discovering the new activity an adventure in and of itself for the children. For example, hide activity materials around the playroom, let the kids unearth them as they play, and then watch the adventure unfold.

- *Use books and songs.*

  We've included a list of related books and songs in each activity that you can use to introduce the activity to the kids (or to support their play and learning after the activity).

- *Experiment with Mystery Words.*

  Use the ideas outlined in chapter 1: Mystery Word (page 1) to introduce vocabulary that will lead the children into an activity.

What are kids learning while they play?

Children's learning is heavily influenced by their past experiences—the knowledge, understanding, and skills they bring to their play—so we can't simply itemize everything an individual child will learn from each activity in this book. What we can tell you, though, is the learning the children might naturally encounter during each one of the activities. The thing is, whereas adults like to sort and classify learning into orderly systems, kids learn all kinds of things all the time. For example, a pair of young children playing with a box of toothpicks and a pile of clay are developing physical skills, social skills, personal skills, math skills, language skills, and thinking skills. Don't worry, kids are wired to learn through play, so if you trust them, follow their lead, and let them play, all sorts of learning will happen. For a deeper understanding of the learning taking place when children play, check out the learning term glossary on page 165.

How can I best support child-led play?

Here are a few big ideas:

- *Nurture.*
  Children who feel safe, secure, and loved possess the foundation they need for play and learning. Kids who do not feel safe, secure, and loved are stressed and have a hard time opening up to the possibilities of play.

- *Know.*
  It is so important to know a child's likes and dislikes in order to successfully inspire her in a fun way. Create an environment that allows you to know the children and their interests very well.

- *Practice.*
  Letting kids lead takes practice. Practice being on your toes and ready to let the kids take the play in an entirely different and spontaneous direction than you might have prepared for. Try letting children lead in these four ways: task, time, team, and technique.

  - *Task.* When kids take charge of selecting the activities they engage in, their brains are more tuned in and focused. We would all rather do what we're interested in than what someone tells us to be interested in.

- *Time.* Children need ample time to settle into play. It's best for adults to set aside our rigid schedules and to operate on kid time.
- *Team.* Allowing children to choose who they interact with is another way to support child-led play. Let's face it: we're all happier, more engaged, and more eager to try new things when we're surrounded by people we enjoy being with.
- *Technique.* Letting kids decide *how* they're going to do what they're doing is another way to trust kids as learners. A child's approach to an activity or task may not be as orderly or straightforward as yours, but early learning is more about the journey than the destination. Trust.

- *Trust.*

  Letting kids lead requires trust. Trusting kids as able, thoughtful, and eager learners creates a solid foundation for play-based learning. Trusting kids means giving them some control over their learning. Realize that children know what they're interested in and have an innate understanding of their own abilities. When you do, you'll be able to trust them to learn.

- *Make room.*

  Kids need room to move in because play is oftentimes a full-body activity. Too often, early learning settings are cramped and cluttered. Big, wide-open, and flexible spaces are best for early learning.

- *Prepare for cleanup.*

  Mess is something that scares a lot of adults away from some activities. Instead of forgoing the activity because you dread the cleanup, prepare for the cleanup ahead of time. For example, have a hand-washing bucket nearby so kids can rinse off their fingers (and other body parts), have the broom or some wet rags handy, or haul the trash can from the kitchen to the activity area. If you prepare for the mess, then it won't be so hard to deal with when the play is done.

Where do I get the ingredients?

You can pick up most of the ingredients (that is, the materials) for these activities at places you're probably already shopping—the local grocery store, a big-box store, a home center, or a dollar store.

Should we document our play experiences?

Yes! Keep a camera, a video camera, or a digital audio recorder nearby to capture the children's play and learning moments. Then share the fun (and learning) with families and use the documentation to assess each child's developmental level. Be sure to note anything you see that raises a red flag (things like speech problems, vision problems, hearing problems, and coordination problems, for example) and follow up on it. Sometimes these things are more noticeable when you watch the instant replay than they are when they're live.

So let's play!

We hope you enjoy the activities in *Let's Play*, but what we really hope you take away from this book is the desire to play more. We hope you see that simple materials, simple prep, and a lot of time, space, and freedom lead to big learning. We also hope the adventures we share inspire brand-new play ideas and variations. If they do, we would love to hear about them. Visit us at www.facebook.com/LetThemPlayBook.

Mystery
Word

This idea comes from our early learning buddy Jenn's busy brain. Lots of kids love solving mysteries, so the idea of a Mystery Word will be very exciting to them. Mystery Word is an active way to build letter recognition, vocabulary, cooperation, and problem-solving skills. We put this activity first because it can be easily integrated into all the activities that follow.

Process

First, some prep work:

1. Create a set of letters—write one letter per index card until you have the whole alphabet.
2. Make duplicates of popular letters so you'll be prepared for any Mystery Word that pops up.
3. File the cards in your index card file box.

Ingredients

❑ 4- x 6-inch index cards
❑ Marker
❑ Index card file box (optional, but it makes for easy storage of your words and letters)

Now share your first Mystery Word with the kids:

1. Choose a word. Make it a fresh, new, fun, or exciting word that relates somehow to what has been going on (or will be going on) in the lives of the kids. For example, here are some popular words from Denita's program: *stomp, slimy, absorb, snot, aim, wow, jump, treasure, dig, imagine, construct, ramp, goopy, string.*

2. Write the word down on a blank index card, and then display the card. You can tape it to the wall, put it in a picture frame, or set it on an activity table—whatever works for your program.

3. From your index card file box, grab the individual letters that spell the word you've chosen, and then hide the letters around the room.

4. Wait for the children to discover the letters and build the word during free play. (There is not a scheduled Mystery Word time.) As their play evolves, the children will discover the letters, and the word will eventually get built.

5. Once the children have found all the letters, let them figure out what the word is.

6. Have the children co-operatively share what they know about letter sounds and try to figure out the word. Younger children need assistance, which older children are more than happy to provide. Give children the opportunity to ask for what they need. Never step in to help until they ask. Figuring out the word can take  time, patience, and persistence—all good skills to practice.

7. Once the children have figured it out, talk about the word. The children will want to share what they know about it. Make time for this Mystery Word conversation with the group and with individual children.

8. Be prepared for play possibilities the Mystery Word may inspire. The children will often incorporate the word into their play. For example, if the Mystery Word is gloppy, you had better be prepared for some messy play.

The Mystery Word concept teaches children letters in a fun, exciting, motivating way. It helps them learn letters, as well as the purpose of each letter, in a very unthreatening, unforced, playful way. All the children feel a sense of pride when they find a letter, and when the younger children ask the older children to assist them in identifying a letter, the older children feel a huge boost of self-esteem. For them, sharing what they know is empowering.

As the letters are found, the children have to construct the Mystery Word by putting letters in the correct order. Doing this is great for learning visual tracking, problem solving, letter sounds, letter recognition, teamwork, ownership of discoveries, knowledge sharing, and community building. Many times, one mystery word builds on another. For example, the word *apart* may lead to the word *together*, and that may lead to the word *attach*, and that may lead to the word *glue*. This means kids are identifying connections between words, stretching and owning their own vocabularies, and actively thinking about language.

More Play Adventures

- *Lowercase letters.* If you've been using all capital letters, use the Mystery Word as a time to introduce lowercase letters. Just write the word in lowercase letters, and then write and hide a matching set of lowercase letters.

- *Match lowercase letters with uppercase letters.* Write the Mystery Word in either uppercase or lowercase letters, and then hide the *opposite* type of letters. The children then have to match the uppercase letters with their lowercase partners, or vice versa.

- *Extra letters.* In addition to the letters needed to build the Mystery Word, hide letters that are *not* part of the word. Then the kids have to figure out which ones belong and which ones do not.

- *Letter scatter.* Instead of hiding the letters, scatter them all over the floor and let the children go on a letter hunt. Call out the letters as they are needed to build the Mystery Word, but do not provide a visual aid. This provides a great way to assess the children's knowledge of letters in a fun, nonthreatening way. Make good observations of the children who are successful as well as those who are not. Don't stand there with a clipboard making checkmarks, just pay attention to who seems to know what. Stay in the moment with them. You can always record anything that needs recording later.

- *Problem solving.* If you hide letters in very tricky and inconvenient places, it takes some problem solving to retrieve them. It's fun to watch the gears turn as children work together to figure out how to get a letter that's been taped to the ceiling.

- *Go magnetic.* Hide magnetic letters instead, and have the children build the word on a refrigerator, metal cabinet, or magnetic marker board.

- *Grab some books or sing.* Share books and songs that are related to the Mystery Word you've selected.

Related Books and Songs

- *Alphabet Mystery* by Audrey Wood
- *Alphabet City* by Stephen T. Johnson
- *The Boy Who Loved Words* by Roni Schotter
- *Max's Words* by Kate Banks
- *Big Words for Little People* by Jamie Lee Curtis
- *The Extinct Alphabet Book* by Jerry Pallotta (Jerry Pallotta's alphabet books are amazing and full of fun words for building vocabularies.)
- "Here Come the ABCs" by They Might Be Giants
- "ABC" by The Jackson 5

_____

_____

_____

_____

_____

_____

_____

Choose your next adventure: turn the page to play with clay, or go to page 44 and splash away.

Natural Clay Play

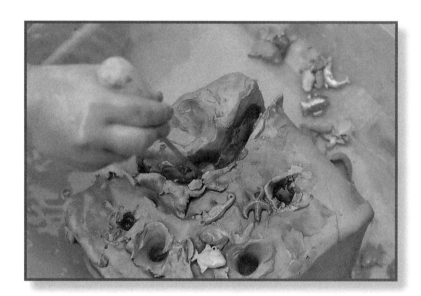

Have you ever run your hands over a 25-pound clump of smooth, wet, natural clay? Denita was thirty-nine years old before she had such an opportunity, and the minute she touched that cool sliminess, she knew her child care crew would *love* it. The ease of cleanup and the re-play potential just added to its desirability. In their play, kids will build small-muscle control, visual tracking skills, social skills, and more.

Process

1. Plop the clay in the shallow tote and wait for a crowd of kids to gather and start asking questions.
2. Add some water to the tote.
3. Demonstrate how to slice hunks from the glob by holding the plastic lacing like dental floss and using a slight sawing motion while pushing down on the clay.

4. Step back, put on your facilitator hat, and let them play. (*Note:* Be considerate of the kids who need to wash their hands frequently because of sensory issues—and of the ones who think playing in the hand-washing bucket is just as much fun as the clay.)

5. When the children are done playing, cleanup is a cinch. Water and rags will clean up any clay mess, and you have two options for storing the clay. If you will use it again soon, wrap the clay snugly in a plastic bag, which will keep it moist and ready to go. If you will not use it again soon, leave the clay open to the air, which will cause it to dry into hard pieces. Then, when you do want to use it again, rehydrate it. Rehydration time will vary by type of clay. We recommend reading through some of the online clay and pottery forums for more clay ideas, tips, and tricks.

Ingredients

❑ 25-pound clump of natural clay (*Note:* Gray clay is less messy, but the red makes great "chocolate milk.") Most hobby stores carry the stuff.

❑ Large, shallow tote (an under-the-bed storage tote works great)

❑ 3 feet of plastic lacing (for cutting the clay)

❑ Water (to keep the clay moist)

❑ Hand-washing bucket with water

More Play Adventures

- *Add some tools.* Try things like forks, spoons, knives, ice cream scoops, long-handled cheese graters, cookie cutters, chopsticks, scissors, hammers, large rocks (for pounding), bowls, cups, putty knives, spatulas, or string.

- *Add some doodads.* Try things like beads, buttons, Legos, toy dinosaurs, toy bugs, pipe cleaners, wooden blocks, toy cars, fuzzy pom-poms, bits of fabric, or hunks of leather.

- *Add some mess.* Try things like baking soda and vinegar, liquid watercolor, ices cubes, or glitter.

- *Rehydrate dry clay.* It's an amazing process. Let the kids add water to hunks of completely dry clay and then watch the hunks turn back into wet clay. Or instead of rehydrating random hunks of dry clay, have the kids make sculptures with wet clay, let the sculptures dry completely, and *then* add water to rehydrate.

- *Make beads.* You must use bakeable polymer clay for this, not natural clay. (It comes in lots of cool colors and is easy to find online.) There are two easy ways

Denita's First Clay Adventure

I chose a gorgeous, windy summer day to plop a chunk of natural clay for the first time. I prepared silently for the new experience and had an instant following of curious *I-want-to-help*ers. It took a lot of muscle for the kids to carry out 25 pounds of clay. I carried out the purple hand-washing bucket, which was half-full of warm, soapy water. One child carried the sensory bin. A few others carried the tools. Another got the hose.

We plopped the clay into the tote with a splash, and I took a 3-foot piece of plastic lacing out of my pocket, held it like dental floss, and proceeded to cut the clay into chunks. It was at this moment that the first question came, quickly followed by a chorus of more: "What is this?" "Can we touch it?" "What's it feel like?" "What can we do with it?" "Can we throw it?" "Can we eat it?" "Have you ever seen anything like this before?"

We discussed what this enticing gray blob was, and then I stepped out of the way. A Denita too close to the action tends to be a Denita offering ideas and making suggestions. I wanted the children to completely own the discoveries I was certain they would make.

Turns were taken, tools were shared, holes were drilled, volcanoes were built, islands were constructed, discoveries *were* made, and learning happened.

By stepping back, *observing*, and not offering my own ideas, I handed ownership of the clay experience to the children. They were overjoyed with their creations, and the play continued the entire morning.

to make beads. You can roll small pieces of clay into balls and pierce them with a large needle, or you can roll the clay into a long snake, cut it into slices, and pierce the slices with a large needle. Once you've made your beads, follow the baking instructions that come with the clay.
- *Fire natural clay.* Natural clay must be fired at high temperatures to maintain its shape and not melt when it gets wet. If you're feeling adventurous, you can

build a homemade kiln (go online to find building plans), or you can learn how to pit-fire or smoke-fire clay. It's a bit of work but would be an excellent play and learning adventure. You could also contact local studios and colleges to see if they could fire your projects.

Related Books and Songs

- *Modeling Clay Animals: Easy-to-Follow Projects in Simple Steps* by Bernadette Cuxart
- *Create Anything with Clay* by Sherri Haab and Laura Torres
- *When Clay Sings* by Byrd Baylor
- *Mudworks: Creative Clay, Dough, and Modeling Experiences* by MaryAnn F. Kohl
- *The Ball of Clay That Rolled Away* by Elizabeth Lenhard
- "Clay Doll (Ni Wa Wa)" by The Shanghai Restoration Project
- "Water, Sand, Blocks, and Clay" by Brady Rymer
- "Sand, Silt, and Clay" by Learning Thru Music

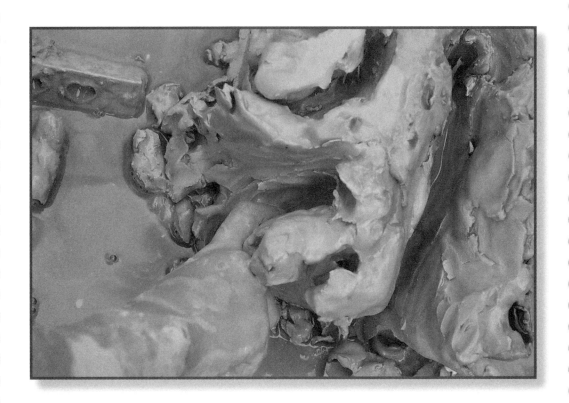

_____

_____

_____

_____

_____

_____

_____

_____

Choose your next adventure: see the next page to make a giant mess, or go to page 79 for a mess that is less.

Big Sensory Play

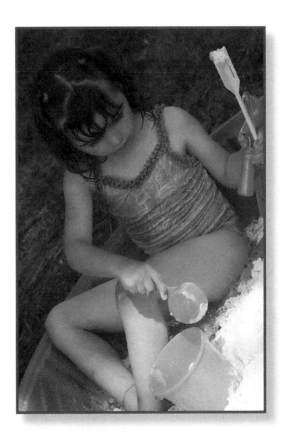

Kids are often eager to experience the world with their whole bodies. They want to feel the colorful goopy stuff, the mud, or the ice-cold water with their toes as well as their fingers. They want to practically climb inside the vinegar-and-baking-soda concoction so they can see it, smell it, feel it, hear it, and taste it up close. They want to use their whole bodies to fully engage with the materials. The problem is, big sensory experiences—and the learning that goes with big sensory experiences—are often stymied by adults. Whole-body activity is valuable for lots of reasons. For example, it strengthens muscles, improves coordination, and develops spatial and kinesthetic awareness. It is also an important pre-writing skill, because core and large-muscle control develop before small-muscle control. Yes, it takes more prep time, it's messy, and it takes more time to clean up. But we want you to go big. Offer kids full-throttle, full-body sensory play. It's awesome, big-time, eyeballs-deep-in-play fun.

Process

1. Add flour, water (less water equals doughier dough, more water equals slimy mess), and liquid watercolor to wading pool.
2. Let kids climb into the pool and play. (Swimsuits are perfect attire for this kind of big play.) Some children may prefer to sit around the pool's edge to play at first. They may change their minds and climb in later.
3. Add water and/or more or different liquid watercolors as desired. You can also add other materials—sand, coffee grounds, potting soil, shredded paper, and so on—to change the experience.
4. When everyone is played out, clean up. A garden hose and a bucket of warm, soapy water come in handy.

Ingredients

❑ Plastic wading pool
❑ 40–60 pounds of flour
❑ Water
❑ Liquid watercolor
❑ Play props—spoons, cups, rags, spatulas, and so forth

Don't Stymie Big Play!

Too often, adults get in the way of big play.

- We place the materials in small totes and then spend the next hour admonishing the children: "Keep it in the tote!" "Don't make such a big mess!" "Not on your face!"

- Because of budget, prep time, and other perfectly reasonable restrictions, we limit the amount of stuff we give children to experience. Two cans of shaving cream are not enough for a group of twelve kids. Two cans may not be enough for *one* kid.

- We don't actually let the children touch the stuff. Glopping some mud in a freezer bag, zipping it shut, and taping it to a table for a kid to poke at is a half-hearted attempt at sensory play.

More Play Adventures

- *Make mud.* Instead of flour, use either soil from your yard or potting soil.
- *Make it fizz.* Let kids climb into the pool and play with baking soda, vinegar, and liquid watercolor.
- *Have fun with shreds.* Add shredded paper and water to the pool and let the play begin.
- *Try full-body painting.* What would happen if you let swimsuit-clad kids climb into a wading pool and fingerpaint themselves? What if you added glitter?

Related Books and Songs

- *Ooey Gooey Handbook: Identifying and Creating Child-Centered Environments* by Lisa Murphy
- *Ooey Gooey Tooey: 140 Exciting Hands-on Activity Ideas for Young Children* by Lisa Murphy
- *Even More Fizzle, Bubble, Pop & WOW!: Simple Science Experiments for Young Children* by Lisa Murphy
- *My Five Senses* by Aliki
- *My Five Senses* by Margaret Miller

- *Look, Listen, Taste, Touch, and Smell: Learning about Your Five Senses* by Pamela Hill Nettleton
- *Sloppy Joe* by Dave Keane
- *Little Blue and Little Yellow* by Leo Lionni
- "Five Senses" by Music with Mar
- "Blending Song" by Music with Mar
- "Colors in Motion" (extended version) by Hap Palmer

Notes

_____

_____

_____

_____

_____

_____

_____

_____

Choose your next adventure: see the next page for worms that wiggle, or go to page 116 and play with a squiggle.

Fun with Worms

Fun with Worms will teach you how to start and maintain a worm farm. You may be thinking, "I've lived my whole life without raising worms. Why should I start now?"

Well, this is a great way to recycle some of your lunch leftovers and to create an ongoing opportunity for kids to learn about physical science, responsibility, caretaking, problem solving, cause-and-effect relationships, and much more. Worm farming will also keep your favorite angler stocked with bait, your pet turtle's tummy full, and your prize rose bush well nourished. Plus, having a big tote of worms writhing around in your basement or garage increases your social standing. (Maybe not with adults, but three-year-olds will love you.) If we still haven't convinced you to give it a try, just think about all the fun you'll have teaching kids to say the word *vermicomposting,* and how much you'll enjoy the look on the faces of parents when kids shout, "Today we harvested worm poop from the vermicomposting bin!"

Process

Get the kids involved in all the steps of this process:

1. Order your worms. Start with five hundred to a thousand of them.
2. Drill a bunch of holes in the bottom of one tote for drainage and a bunch of holes in the tote lid for ventilation.
3. Find a fairly cool and dark place for your worm bin to live. Basements and garages are good choices. You want a place that maintains a fairly constant temperature all year long—your worms will be happiest when the temperature is 55–75 degrees.
4. Place the second (hole-less) tote on the floor, put the bricks inside it, and then put the drilled tote on top of the bricks. The bricks raise the second tote, allowing the bottom tote to catch excess moisture that might drip from the top tote and improving air circulation. Fill the top tote about three-quarters full of moist but not soggy shredded paper.
5. On top of the paper, add pieces of moist but not soggy cardboard to cover the entire surface.
6. As soon as they arrive, lay your worms under the moist but not soggy cardboard in the top tote.
7. Feed the worms a little food every week or so. They love veggies and fruits and breads. Avoid meats and dairy, because worms don't like them and your vermicomposting adventure will get icky and smelly. Lay bits of food in the shredded paper, but not too much—start

Ingredients

- ❑ 2 large (10 gallon-ish) opaque plastic nesting totes and one lid (They can't be translucent because the worms need dark.)
- ❑ Drill with a 1/8-inch bit
- ❑ A couple of bricks
- ❑ Shredded paper (newspaper, office paper, and craft paper work fine. Avoid glossy paper.)
- ❑ Lunch scraps (no meat, no dairy)
- ❑ Water
- ❑ Cardboard
- ❑ Worms (You can't use just any old worms. Red wigglers are the best worms for composting, and you can find them online.)

with a cup or so; too much food leads to nasty smells. As your worm population grows, you can feed it more.

Your worms are like Goldilocks—they're happiest when things are *just right*: not too hot and not too cold, not too wet and not too dry, not too much food and not too little. It is hard to underfeed them and easy to overfeed them. We recommend searching online for an active vermicomposting forum. There are a lot of folks out on the web who love talking worms and will be eager to offer help and suggestions—especially if they know kids are involved in the caretaking.

Over time, the worms will digest the shredded paper and cardboard, so you will need to add more. Jeff has had his worms for years, and they are happiest when they have a food-to-paper ratio of about one to eight. The liquid from the food you add tends to keep the paper moist enough, but if you find that it's getting a bit too dry, you can add some water. The excess will drain into the lower tote. If you find that Goldilocks sweet spot, you'll probably notice an increase in worm population in a few months.

More Play Adventures

- *Sensory play.* Place a few dozen worms in a sensory tote and let the kids handle them. Just make sure to add some of the moist but not soggy shredded-paper bedding to help keep them damp and happy. Magnifying glasses offer a fun way to explore these little critters.

- *Feed plants.* As your worm bin becomes established, a layer of compost slowly forms on the bottom of the tote. Have the kids help harvest this black gold by sorting through it to remove the worms and undigested bits of paper and food and then adding it to house or garden plants.
- *Practice caretaking.* Schedule regular times for worm caretaking. Worms can help kids learn lots about selflessness, nurturing, and responsibility.
- *Go small.* Not ready to start your own worm farm? Just go to the local bait shop, buy a few dozen worms, and let the kids get to know them.
- *Try other critters.* If you have access to a well-stocked bait shop, you can also let the kids get to know minnows and leeches. These critters are easy to care for. You can find instructions online. Once you're done with the critters, you can donate them to your favorite angler.

Related Books and Songs

- *Worms Eat My Garbage: How to Set Up and Maintain a Worm Composting System* by Mary Appelhof (This book has good information for kids and adults.)
- *Diary of a Worm* by Doreen Cronin
- *Wonderful Worms* by Linda Glaser
- *Wiggling Worms at Work* by Wendy Pfeffer
- *Compost Stew* by Mary McKenna Siddals
- *An Earthworm's Life* by John Himmelman
- *Composting: Nature's Recyclers* by Robin Koontz
- "Wiggle Worm" by Music with Mar
- "Inchworm" by Danny Kaye
- "Glow Worm," made famous by The Mills Brothers
- "Wiggle" by Peter Alsop
- Search vermicomposting online for all the info you could ever want on the topic.

Notes

Choose your next adventure: turn the page for giant dough, or go to page 26 and see things glow.

Monster-Sized Playdough

Playdough is fun. A great big monster-sized hunk of playdough is more fun. And a great big monster-sized hunk of playdough full of monster parts is *really* fun. It's *really* packed full of learning too. Manipulating a huge chunk of playdough requires lots of muscles working together. Finger muscles, tired from the work of so much playdough, often recruit fists, forearms, and elbows to dig, roll, pound, and shape. Monster-sized playdough is a whole-body activity: big muscles in the arms and chest pull and push, tongues stick out, and facial muscles scrunch. Feeling your arms buried to the elbow in playdough is also a sensory moment like no other—unless you decide to let your toes in on the action. Monster-sized playdough is also rich in pre-literacy learning (seeing positive and negative space, for example) and pre-math skills (the explorations of size, shape, and quantities, for example). Last but not least, monster-sized playdough is also great for hiding things, for discovering, and for inspiring imaginations. Read the ideas below and then follow the lead of your creative crew to inspire even more fantastic, monster-sized playdough adventures!

Process

1. Mix the googly eyes, golf tees, pipe cleaners, craft sticks, and any other monster parts into four batches of homemade playdough.

2. Plop it all on a table in one huge heap.

3. Step back and be amazed by how the children choose to manipulate such a large mass of playdough, how they share it, work together, argue (which enhances vocabulary and builds good debating skills), reason, and just plain enjoy the freedom so much playdough allows.

4. As they play, someone will probably decide golf tees look like sharp teeth or that craft sticks are legs, and monster building will commence. If it doesn't, that's fine, too—just go with the flow.

Ingredients

- ❑ At least four batches of colored homemade playdough (Get creative: your playdough monsters can be any color. See page 23 for our favorite playdough recipes.)
- ❑ Googly eyes
- ❑ Golf tees
- ❑ Pipe cleaners
- ❑ Colored craft sticks
- ❑ Any other "monster parts" you want to try

- *Pirate treasure playdough.* Brown, dirt-colored playdough works great for this variation. Just hide a selection of beaded necklaces, plastic jewels, golden coins, plastic skulls, or rubber bugs and snakes (use caution with children prone to putting objects in their mouth). Have a treasure chest handy in which to stow the collected treasure. Consider making a giant graph to see how many of each item the kids find. This activity is even more fun if everyone wears an eye patch.

- *Paleontologist playdough.* Again, a large mound of brown play dough works great for this variation. Collect some real bones—steak bones, ham bones, turkey bones, and large chicken bones work great. Clean them thoroughly, let them dry for a few weeks, spray them with a bleach solution, and let them dry again before adding them to your playdough. Then have tweezers, toothpicks, and old toothbrushes available for extracting the bones and cleaning off the playdough. (Toy bones and dinosaurs work for this activity if you don't want to prep your own real bones.)

- *Gross playdough.* Mix up four batches of playdough in four different colors. Then hide stretchy, rubbery gummy bugs, spiders, snakes, or frogs in the playdough and let the kids mix it up. After it is all mixed up, hand out scissors and let them snip away. If you really want to make it gross, start adding water to the dough a teaspoon at a time until it turns into a slimy mess.

- *Rainbow playdough.* Make three batches of playdough—one red, one yellow, and one blue. Put it all together on the table and challenge the kids to figure out how to make the missing rainbow colors: green, purple, and orange. To extend the rainbow play, add leprechauns, gold coins, real flowers, tiny toy unicorns, or other fancy fantasy-related props.

- *Halloween playdough.* Make two batches of yellow playdough and two batches of red playdough and then plop them on the table so the kids can start mixing. It may take a few days of good, solid play for the colors to transform to orange. No matter how many times you mix colors, children are excited when they discover the change occurring. As they mix, you can add various items to the playdough—perhaps tiny plastic pumpkins, cats, bats, or even cleaned, dried pumpkin seeds.

- *Leprechaun playdough.* Make two batches of blue and two batches of yellow playdough. Place all the batches in a giant container with a note on it from a leprechaun expressing his disappointment that he can't find his green playdough. For even more fun, type the note on the computer using a tiny font size, so a magnifying glass is necessary to read it. As the children play, the missing green playdough will appear—make sure to write the leprechaun a

Playdough Recipes

Here are two playdough recipes we like, based on recipes from Lisa "The Ooey Gooey Lady" Murphy. The first is our favorite—we like the way it feels. The directions are the same for both of them; only the ingredients differ slightly. So pick one list of ingredients and follow the directions below for either recipe to make your playdough.

Lotion Playdough

- ❑ 3 cups flour
- ❑ 3 tablespoons powdered or granulated alum
- ❑ 3/4 cup salt
- ❑ 6 tablespoons vegetable oil
- ❑ 3 cups water plus liquid watercolor (as part of the 3 cups of water)
- ❑ 1 cup inexpensive, scented baby lotion
- ❑ Bowl
- ❑ Electric mixer or hand whisk
- ❑ Sturdy spatula

Basic Playdough

- ❑ 3 cups flour
- ❑ 1 1/2 cups salt
- ❑ 6 teaspoons cream of tartar
- ❑ 6 tablespoons vegetable oil
- ❑ 3 cups water plus liquid watercolor (as part of the 3 cups of water)
- ❑ Bowl
- ❑ Electric mixer or hand whisk
- ❑ Sturdy spatula

Directions:

1. Mix all ingredients together in a bowl.
2. Stir while cooking over medium heat in a saucepan until dough forms a ball. As the playdough stiffens, flip it over so the mushy stuff gets to the heat.
3. Once it's formed a clump, place playdough on a table and knead until it feels properly playdoughy (if it's a little sticky, add a couple tablespoons of flour while kneading).
4. Place in an open ziplock bag until it has cooled completely; moisture forms if you put it in a closed container too soon, and it gets quite sticky. If you have some little helping hands around, you can let the kids play with the warm dough while it cools—just make sure it is not too hot when you give it to them. The next time you bring out the playdough, it will be ready for one of our play suggestions.

note letting him know you found it. As the days progress and the children continue to play with the dough, add shamrock confetti or other fun green items to extend the play.

Related Books and Songs

- *If You're A Monster and You Know It* by Ed and Rebecca Emberley
- *Glad Monster, Sad Monster* by Ed Emberley and Anne Miranda
- *Go Away, Big Green Monster!* by Ed Emberley
- *There Was an Old Monster* by Rebecca, Adrian, and Ed Emberley
- *Tickle Monster* by Josie Bissett
- *Where the Wild Things Are* by Maurice Sendak
- *The Gruffalo* by Julie Donaldson
- *How I Became a Pirate* by Melinda Long
- *On a Pirate Ship* by Sarah Courtauld
- *Shiver Me Letters: A Pirate ABC* by June Sobel
- *Pirates Don't Change Diapers* by Melinda Long
- *What Makes a Rainbow: A Magic Ribbon Book* by Betty Ann Schwartz
- *A Color of His Own* by Leo Lionni
- *Is This a Monster?* by Scarlett Lovell and Diane Snowball
- "Are You a Pirate?" by Denita Dinger (sung to the tune of "I'm a Little Teapot," with the following lyrics)

  Arrrrrgh you a pirate or a captain crunch?
  Arrrrrgh you ready for a pirate's lunch?
  Grab a slice of cheese and a chunk of lumpy green
  It's the most disgusting thing that you've ever seen!

- "The Monster" by Music with Mar
- "Monster Day" by Linda Arnold
- "Ghostbusters" by Ray Parker Jr.
- "Let's Make Play-Dough!" by Miss Jenny & Friends
- "Let's Play with Playdough" by Kath Bee
- "Playdough" by The Candy Band

Notes

_____

_____

_____

_____

_____

_____

_____

_____

Choose your next adventure: turn the page for play in the dark, or go to page 54 for a toy with bark.

An Activity That Will Glow on You

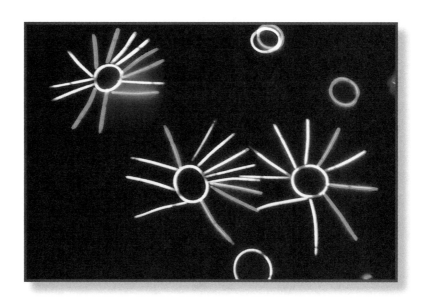

Oh, the play and learning treasures you can find for just *one dollar*! One-dollar treasures aren't always easy to find, but keep your eyes open, and you'll discover them. Glow sticks are a wonderful play-and-learning one-dollar treasure, so grab as many as you can when you come across them. They're good for play anytime but are ideal on dreary, rainy days when outdoor play is a challenge. Just pull the blinds, cut the lights, and start the glowing fun! Don't see the learning right away? Look closer, and you'll see kids developing large- and small-muscle skills, honing social skills, problem solving, and much more.

Process

1. Come up with a fun way for the kids to discover the glow sticks. Have a few of them out and already glowing when the kids arrive, perhaps laced around the necks of a few stuffed animals, or hanging in the coat closet where the jackets go. Wear a lovely

glow-stick necklace while you greet the children in the morning!

2. Discuss safety with the kids. Show them how dark the room will become when the lights are turned out. Ask them to name some things they can do safely when the room is dark. Focus on the *can dos*: We *can* create, we *can* have fun, we *can* move slowly, and so on. Don't make it a big deal. Keep the safety discussion short and simple.

3. Hit the lights and let them play. Let the play continue for as long as interest is there. (This could be hours for some kids.)

4. Go big with glow stick play. Each child will need at least four—one for each hand and foot.

Ingredients

- ❑ Glow sticks (Denita generally starts off with 75 glow sticks for the 12 kids in her program.)
- ❑ A dark room
- ❑ Plenty of time
- ❑ Plenty of space

More Play Adventures

- *Set aside the connectors that accompany the glow sticks.* (These are the pieces used to hold the glow sticks in a circle for bracelets or necklaces.) Before play starts, put all the little connectors in a couple of bowls and save them for later. After the kids have played with the glow sticks for a while, put the bowls where someone will discover them. This is a good way to extend play.

Don't *Hoard* Them. *Use* Them!

After you snag a great deal on a bunch of glow sticks, *use them*. That's what they're for! No one learns anything or has any fun when the glow sticks—or the markers, the paint, the glue, or the glitter, for that matter—sit unused on a shelf or in a tote. Too often, caregivers and teachers stash fun stuff like glow sticks away. Then, after thirty years of working with kids, they retire and sell it all at a garage sale. Don't be that person. Don't lock the fun stuff away for later. Use your supplies. Get your play on.

- *Make it darker.* Use blankets, clothespins, cardboard sheets, and duct tape to create a cozy dark space in your playroom. This space is especially good for those kids who want to continue the glow-stick play after the rest of the group has moved on.
- *Play after the glow.* Keep the glow sticks around even after the glow is gone. Kids still like to build things with the tubes and connectors.
- *Add some mirrors.* Provide some mirrors so kids can watch themselves spin and twist the glowing sticks.
- *Combine them with other things.* Try glow sticks and playdough play, glow sticks and water play, glow sticks and mud, glow sticks and a light table, or glow sticks in balloons.

Related Books and Songs

- *What Was I Scared Of? A Glow-in-the Dark Encounter* by Dr. Seuss
- *The Day-Glo Brothers: The True Story of Bob and Joe Switzer's Bright Ideas and Brand-New Colors* by Chris Barton
- *Glow-in-the-Dark Constellations: A Field Guide for Young Stargazers* by C. E. Thompson
- *Janice VanCleave's Chemistry for Every Kid: 101 Easy Experiments That Really Work* by Janice VanCleave
- "I Saw the Light" by Hank Williams
- "These Little Stars of Mine" by Music with Mar
- "Glow Worm" by The Mills Brothers

_____

_____

_____

_____

_____

_____

_____

_____

Choose your next adventure: turn the page for custom block stacking or go to page 75 and see why boxes are for more than packing.

Peanut Butter Jar Blocks

Peanut butter jar blocks offer an easy and economical way to energize your block and dramatic play areas while also introducing concepts like color and weight and letters and numbers. The curious contents of your peanut butter jar blocks will engage kids of all ages. Curious infants and toddlers will enjoy shaking, toting, and rolling them. Older kids will stack and build with them in the block area and use them to hold potions and medicines during dramatic play.

Process

1. Clean the peanut butter jars and remove the labels.
2. Put a few sensory items into each jar: small blocks, paper clips, toy dinosaurs, toy cars.
3. Add a few drops of superglue to the jar's threads and screw on the lid.
4. Let the glue set up.
5. Add the new peanut butter jar blocks to your play area so kids can discover them.

Ingredients

- ❏ Empty plastic peanut butter jars and lids
- ❏ Sensory stuff from around the house (for example, bird seed, Hot Wheels cars, Lego bricks, coins, rocks, crayons, or those little plastic green soldiers) to put into the jars
- ❏ Superglue

More Play Adventures

- *Counting blocks.* You'll need eleven jars and fifty-five of the same somethings. The somethings can be most anything: craft sticks, clothes pins, wooden matchsticks, quarters, stones, marbles, or bouncy balls. Any little thing you happen to have fifty-five of will work fine. Now, place zero somethings in one jar, one something in another jar, two somethings in the next jar, and so on—until you have eleven jars containing zero to ten somethings. After the lids are glued on, you can let the children play.

- *Alphabet blocks.* You'll need twenty-six jars, a set of letters (cut them yourself from card stock or use small foam, plastic, or wood letters), and twenty-six items. Give each jar a letter and a related object—for instance, A and plastic ants, B and a pack of bubble gum, and C and a couple toy cars—before gluing on the lids.

- *Color blocks.* Grab a few jars, some water, and some food coloring (or liquid watercolor). Fill each jar about half-full of water, add color, glue on the lids, and play. You can bling them out with some glitter, if you like.
- *Weight blocks.* You'll need three to five jars and an assortment of stuff to put in them. The aim is to create a set of blocks with noticeably different weights. Maybe put a feather in one, a small toy puppy in another, and a bunch of stones in a third.
- *Shape blocks.* Just fill a few jars with different shapes: round things in one jar, triangular things in another, and cubes in a third.
- *Money blocks.* Create a set of blocks that contain different coins: a jar with pennies, a jar with dimes, a jar with nickels, and a jar with quarters, for example.
- *Matching blocks.* Use any of the ideas above, but make two or more of each block, so kids can match them up, as in: "Look! I found two pink-water blocks!"

Related Books and Songs

- *Purple, Green and Yellow* by Robert Munsch
- *Lemonade in Winter: A Book about Two Kids Counting Money* by Emily Jenkins
- *A Circle Here, A Square There: My Shapes Book* by David Diehl
- "We Know Our Shapes" by Music with Mar
- "Going on a Shape Hunt" by Music with Mar
- "De Colores" by Jose-Luis Orozco
- "Colors" by Music with Mar
- "'A' You're Adorable" by Perry Como
- "The ABC's of You" by Red Grammer

Notes

_____

_____

_____

_____

_____

_____

_____

Choose your next adventure: turn the page for painting cooperation, or go to page 1 if words are your inclination.

Marble Painting on Steroids

Marble painting is a common early learning activity usually done by one child at a time. Making it *BIG* turns it into a cooperative effort that requires practicing social skills and self-regulation. It is a very physical activity that builds large and small muscles. Teamwork, cooperation, and learning by trial and error are only a few of its additional benefits. Marble painting on steroids will also provide big boosts of confidence and encourage self-esteem.

Process

1. Line your big box with white paper and secure it in place with some tape.
2. Let the children squeeze paint all over the paper. Not too much, or the paper will get saturated and rip, but don't be stingy with it, either.
3. Add your balls of choice one at a time, all at once, or whatever. Let the kids decide.

The Perfect Big Box

Dumpster dive, beg, steal, or borrow to find the perfect box. A good-quality box will last a long time and can be used for lots of things. In addition to marble painting, Denita's perfect big box has served for years as her program's Lego Zone, as well as its hospital, doctor's office, hair salon, restaurant, and ice cream shop. Jeff's program once had a heavy-duty laser printer box that the kids used every day, and it lasted longer than the printer that came in it. The point is you can't go wrong with a good-quality cardboard box.

4. Let the children figure out how to move the balls around. Let them problem solve through trial and error until they discover a successful method. This is your cue to *be quiet* and *to observe*. Go on, *step away* from the paint-covered balls under the control of young children. Trust them to play and learn. You can do it!

5. After the kids are done, remove the balls and give them a good cleaning. (The kids can and should help with this.)

6. Give your painting plenty of time to dry, remove it from the box, and then display it.

Ingredients

❏ One large box (ideally 6 x 4 x 1 feet, but any large, shallow box will work)
❏ Large paper (butcher paper works great)
❏ Masking tape
❏ Several colors of paint
❏ Balls of all sizes (Marbles, bouncy balls, baseballs, softballs, golf balls, and the like work well. We do not, however, recommend bowling balls. With them things could go horribly wrong.)

More Play Adventures

- *Opt for a pool.* If you haven't found the perfect cardboard box, a ridged wading pool will work fine.
- *Practice first.* Let the kids practice moving the balls around before you put the paper and paint in the box. They'll have a grand time manipulating the box and watching the balls bash and bounce about. Then, after they've done some problem solving and figured out how to manipulate the box, pose a question, such as, "Wouldn't it be fun if the balls left a trail behind them? How could we do that?"

- *Ramp painting.* Instead of moving the box around to set the balls to moving, use ramps. (Plastic rain gutters make great ramps—and see what else you can do with them on page 149.) Set the ramps around the edge of your large paper-lined box so that the balls will plop into it. Have bowls of various paint colors sitting close by. The children can put the balls in the paint, let them roll down the ramp, and watch them skedaddle across the paper—leaving a trail of color behind.

- *Magnet-ball painting.* Make a bridge between two tables using a 10-foot plastic rain gutter. Secure it to each table with some adhesive putty. Pour some paint in the rain gutter and add some 3/4-inch metal ball bearings (available online and at most home center and farm supply stores). Spread the paint around inside the rain gutter by moving magnets under the gutter to manipulate the ball bearings. To extend the play, add smaller ball bearings, small magnets, or paper clips.

The Birth of This Idea

Instead of waiting around for the Cat in the Hat to show up with Thing 1 and Thing 2 on a rainy day, Denita pulled together some toy cars, a clever group of children, a giant box, and *boom*—Marble Painting on Steroids was born. The children figured out that when they put toy cars inside one end of the box and lifted up that end, the cars would roll to the other end. This was no easy task, because the box was so big, awkward, and heavy. As time passed, the kids tried rolling different objects, and eventually someone suggested adding paint.

Be Aware of Bounce-ability

If you do this project inside, be aware of the bounce-ability of the balls you choose. Nothing can add unwanted color to a room faster than a crazed bouncy ball covered in paint, ricocheting off the floor and walls. Be cautious with bigger balls too. They can easily escape the protection of the box and make a real mess.

- *Explore other options.* Instead of ball bearings, use toy cars. Instead of toy cars, use small rocks. Instead of small rocks, try wine corks. Instead of wine corks, try toy dinosaurs.
- *Experiment.* Use different types of paint or different amounts of paint. Use two ball bearings instead of twenty. What if you layer the paint, letting one color dry before adding another? What happens if you use shaving cream instead of paint, or shaving cream *and* paint? How about glitter?

Related Books and Songs

- *The Enormous Carrot* by Vladimir Vagin
- *A Camping Spree with Mr. Magee* by Chris Van Dusen
- *Rolling Harvey Down the Hill* by Jack Prelutsky
- *The Little Red Hen* by Paul Galdone
- *The Little Red Hen (Makes a Pizza)* by Philemon Sturges
- "Pinball Wizard" by The Who
- "Co-Op-Er-Ate" by Music with Mar
- "Little Red Hen" by Music with Mar
- "Roll On Down the Highway" by Bachman-Turner Overdrive
- "Roll Over Beethoven" by Chuck Berry
- Do a Google search for Jackson Pollock images online, show them to the kids, and compare their big marble paintings to his work.

_____

_____

_____

_____

_____

_____

_____

_____

Choose your next adventure: see the next page if you're a marble fanatic, or go to page 104 for play dramatic.

Pool-Noodle Raceway

Pool noodles. They are inexpensive, readily available, durable, and full of fun. Add a few marbles, some tape, and a bit of gravity, and you're in for hours of play-based learning, including development of physical, social, and thinking skills.

Process

1. With the serrated knife, slice the noodles lengthwise down the middle into two long pieces. (Better yet, trust a child to do the cutting.) Try to go right down the middle, but don't worry if your cut drifts a little bit. It does not have to be perfect.

2. Place the noodles side by side with the freshly cut surface facing down.

Ingredients

- ❑ Hollow-core pool noodles—one is enough to get started, but more are better
- ❑ Serrated knife
- ❑ Marbles
- ❑ Duct tape

3. Duct tape the two slices together.

4. Flip them over (cut side up) and securely tape one end to an elevated surface, like a chair or a coffee table, and tape the other end to the floor.

5. With a *Ready . . . Set . . . GO!* show the children how marbles placed in the slot at the upper end of the noodles will race to the floor.

6. Step back and let them play.

More Play Adventures

- *Build longer raceways.* Make lots of sliced noodles and a bunch of masking or duct tape available, and let the kids figure out how to make a raceway that reaches clear across the room. They can connect a series of noodles with tape to create long tracks for the marbles to race along. Aligning the noodles *just so* will take practice and experimentation, but they'll figure it out.

- *Add some hills.* Place a few blocks under the raceway to create hills. How big can the hill get before the marble is unable to get over it?

- *Build a ramp.* Try elevating the lower end of the track by a few inches to create a ramp so the marbles will grab some air when they reach the end of the raceway. How far will the marbles fly? Do the kids need to raise the other end so the marble will have more speed?

- *Build a roller coaster.* Let the kids use a bunch of sliced pool noodles and some duct tape to create their own marble roller coaster runs. They can connect the noodles to one another the long way, then twist, bend, and wrap them around objects like tables, chair legs, fences, deck railings, trees, and ladders,

Marble Safety

Marbles are small, and some kids are prone to putting small stuff in their mouths. A marble-related injury is statistically unlikely, but it's a good idea to take a few simple steps to stay safe:

- *Know how many marbles you started with.* Make sure you put that many marbles away when play is done.
- *Be vigilant.* Know the kids you're working with and keep a closer eye on the ones who are most likely to mouth marbles.
- *Explain that marbles are for playing, not eating.* Don't make it a lecture; just work it into the conversation when you start to play.

and secure them with tape. It will take the children a while to figure out that the slot in the noodle must face up so the marble doesn't fall out; that the noodle needs a certain amount of slope for the marble to roll; and that the marble will hit road bumps and stop if the noodles are not properly aligned. Let the children make these discoveries for themselves; the learning will be more lasting if they do. Step in only if invited or if the children become too frustrated. (A bit of frustration, however, can be a good thing.)

- *Keep track of time.* Use a stopwatch or a stopwatch app to time the marbles as they race along the track. Which marble is the fastest? Take it a step further and record the times of all the marble and use the information to create a graph.
- *Make a ring.* Take a section of the noodle track, loop the ends together with the slot on the inside and form a ring; secure it with duct tape. Now ask the children to place a marble or two inside the slot and see if they can spin the ring so the marble inside travels all the way around the circumference. This is an example of

Test That Hole

Experience taught Jeff that not all marbles and pool-noodle holes play together nicely, so when you shop for *your* pool noodles, take a marble along. While you're in the store, drop it through a noodle hole to make sure it fits. You may look silly to passing shoppers, but a bit of embarrassment is better than marbles that won't roll when it's time to play.

centrifugal force. It's a fun term to teach to kids—and the hands-on experience is more valuable than the fancy word.

- *Makes a noodle block.* Try slicing a pool noodle or two into noodle blocks. Just use a serrated knife to slice the noodles (as you'd slice a cucumber) into pieces about 2 feet long, and there you have it: noodle blocks. Very versatile! Kids can play with them as they would wooden blocks, and they can use them in water play, as lacing beads, and as props in dramatic play. Noodle blocks are safe for throwing, too, which is a great way to build coordination, strengthen small and large muscles, and learn about the physical world. Try pinching them between your thumb and forefinger; they'll *POP* into the air.

Related Books and Songs

- *The Racecar Alphabet* by Brian Floca
- *If I Built a Car* by Chris Van Dusen
- *Forces Make Things Move* by Kimberly Brubaker Bradley
- *Energy Makes Things Happen* by Kimberly Brubaker Bradley
- *The Marble Book* by Richie Chevat
- "Rolling in the Deep (Sleepy Remix)" by Baby Rockstar
- "Rolling Home" by Steven Courtney Band

Notes

_____

_____

_____

_____

_____

_____

_____

_____

Choose your next adventure: turn the page for fun in liquid form, or go to page 82 for an activity beyond the norm.

Splishing, Splashing, Squirting Play Sprinkler

Kids love water play, and water play is a wonderful way for them to learn about the physical world, hone physical and cognitive skills, and practice social skills. Want an easy-to-build, durable, and incredibly fun way to create some big water play? Build this 8-foot-long play sprinkler, slap on your swimsuit, and go play.

Process

1. Prime and glue the pipe cap onto one end of the pipe, following directions included with the PVC cement.
2. Glue the fittings onto the other end of the pipe.

3. Have a cup of coffee or take a nap while you let the PVC cement set up.

4. Drill holes along the length of the pipe every 12 inches or so. You can make them in a straight line on one side of the pipe or you can place the holes randomly around the pipe. (*Note:* The number of holes you can drill will depend a lot on your water pressure.) Start with a few holes and add more if needed. Don't worry: if you end up making too many holes, you can fill them in with silicone caulk.

5. Hook up a garden hose, place the pipe on the ground, turn on the water, and play.

Ingredients

- ❑ One 8-foot piece of 2-inch Schedule 40 PVC pipe
- ❑ One 2-inch Schedule 40 PVC pipe cap
- ❑ Assorted bushings, reducers, and fittings to attach a garden hose to the 2-inch PVC pipe (It's hard to say get *This*, *That*, and *Those* because not all plumbing departments label these bits and pieces with the same names. The best way to assure you get what you need is to tell the plumbing person at your local home center that you want to hook a section of 2-inch PVC pipe to a garden hose—and then let them find you the parts.)
- ❑ PVC primer and cement
- ❑ Drill with 1/16-inch drill bit

More Play Adventures

- *Angle it.* Lean one end of the pipe against a tree or wall. (You can use a bungee cord to secure it.)
- *Hang it.* Suspend the pipe using bungee cords between two trees or across the top bar of a swing set.
- *Dangle it.* Install an eyehook with either a screw or bolt end in the capped end of the pipe, and use the hook to suspend the pipe from a tree branch to create a water-play pendulum (the hose end will be on the bottom).
- *Support it.* Support water play by introducing other water play materials like buckets, sponges, squirt guns, and mud.

Related Books and Songs

- *It's Raining, It's Pouring* by Andrea Spalding
- *Splash!* by Ann Jonas
- *Wet Dog!* by Elise Broach
- *Super Simple Things to Do with Water: Fun and Easy Science for Kids* by Kelly Doudna
- "Swingin' in the Rain" by Maria Muldaur
- "Splish Splash" by Bobby Darin
- "Five Little Ducks" by Little Star Children Choir
- "Puddle Stomping" by Anna Moo
- "Rain, Rain, Go Away" (popular children's song)
- "It's Raining, It's Pouring" (popular children's song)

_____

_____

_____

_____

_____

_____

_____

Choose your next adventure: turn the page for pipe construction, or go to page 66 for fun with suction.

Super-Duper PVC Construction Set

O ne of the most popular projects in Jeff's *Do-It-Yourself Early Learning*, his first book, is the Pipe Construction Set, which consists of 1/2-inch PVC pipe and fittings that kids can use for building. Building with this new Super-Duper PVC Construction Set, which uses 1 1/2-inch PVC pipe and is intended for play outside, is a great way to build children's muscles and imaginations as well as their social skills, self-regulatory skills, pre-numeracy skills, and pre-literacy skills.

Process

1. Cut the straight pieces of pipe into sections between 12 and 36 inches long.
2. Place the straight pipes and connecting pieces in your play area.
3. Wait for kids to discover them and start playing.

Ingredients

- ❏ Four 10-foot pieces of 1 1/2-inch Schedule 40 PVC pipe
- ❏ Assorted 1 1/2-inch Schedule 40 PVC pipe connecting pieces (90° fittings, 45° fittings, straight fittings, and Y fittings)
- ❏ Saw (Most any saw will work.)

More Play Adventures

- *Get wet.* Provide water to pour through the pipes. You can also add some 2-inch valves so the children can control the flow of water through the pipes.
- *Dump sand.* Sand is another material that expands pipe play. Kids in Jeff's program enjoy dumping sand into one end of their pipe structures and then twisting and turning the structures until it comes out the other end.
- *Go bigger.* Build a construction set out of 2-inch or larger pipe. This is an option for older kids. School-age kids will enjoy the bigger pipes—and the bigger structures they can build. Little hands have a hard time putting bigger pipe together, but little kids still love playing with the larger pipe.
- *Build a hideout.* Use the pipe and fittings to make a frame, cover it with a tarp or an old blanket (secure it with duct tape), and play.

Related Books and Songs

- *Plant Plumbing: A Book about Roots and Stems* by Susan Blackaby
- *Plumbers* by Tracey Boraas
- *Steve Caney's Ultimate Building Book Including More Than 100 Incredible Projects Kids Can Make!* by Steven Caney
- *Janice VanCleave's Engineering for Every Kid: Easy Activities That Make Learning Science Fun* by Janice VanCleave
- "Seed to Flower" by Music with Mar

_____

_____

_____

_____

_____

_____

_____

_____

Choose your next adventure: see the next page and make a roller, or go to page 125 for an activity that is nearly polar.

Textured Rollers

Here's a fun way to extend playdough play and help kids develop their pre-reading skills. Learning to see the patterns these rollers will create in a slab of playdough is practice in seeing words on the pages of books. Using the rollers also hones hand-eye coordination and builds small muscles—important pre-reading and pre-writing skills.

Process

1. Slice the dowel into 6-inch to 8-inch sections.
2. Lightly sand the dowel sections. Make sure to ease the edges and smooth the end grain a bit.
3. Wipe the dowel sections down with a dry rag to remove sawdust.
4. Use your hot glue gun to create patterns on the dowel sections: dots, squiggles, zig-zags, squares, triangles, waves, circles, horizontal or vertical lines, letters, numbers,

names—whatever pops into your mind. Work methodically. We suggest decorating a quarter section of a dowel and letting it dry and cool completely before moving on to the next section. This will reduce the chances you'll burn yourself, and it'll keep you from smearing your work.

5. Once the hot glue has completely dried, check over the dowel sections and remove any of those annoying hot glue stringy thingies you find.

6. Get out some playdough and let the kids start rolling, rolling, rolling. (Check out page 23 for our favorite playdough recipes.)

Ingredients

❑ Wooden dowel, 1 1/2 inches in diameter and 36 to 48 inches long
❑ Saw (Any sharp saw will do the job—a handsaw, circular saw, band saw, table saw, or skill saw is a good choice. A chainsaw would be overkill.)
❑ Sandpaper, 100 grit
❑ Rag
❑ Hot glue gun
❑ Hot glue (The plain old translucent stuff is fine, but colored hot glue would be better. Many craft shops carry the stuff, and it's also available online.)

More Play Adventures

- *Make stamps.* Use the techniques above to apply hot glue to flat hunks of wood to create custom stamps. You can use wooden blocks that you already have on hand for this, or you can cut some out of a piece of pine 3/4 inch thick and 2 inches wide. Just cut the wood into blocks about 3 inches long, sand them a bit, and hot-glue a pattern, letter, number, or shape on one side.
- *Have a ball.* Pick up some smallish and smooth-surfaced balls at the dollar store and then hot-glue patterns, shapes, letters, or numbers onto their surface to create textured balls that kids can roll across playdough.

Remember to Reverse Them

If you make letters or numbers on your rollers or stamps, remember to reverse the images so the letters come out facing the correct way on the dough. We suggest creating a cheat sheet to use while gluing by writing the letters or numbers out in reverse on a scrap of paper first.

Related Books and Songs

- *Pattern Fish* by Trudy Harris
- *Pattern Bugs* by Trudy Harris
- *Shapes, Shapes, Shapes* by Tana Hoban
- "Learning Our Shapes" by Twin Sisters Productions
- "Bend Me, Shape Me" by the American Breed

Notes

_____

_____

_____

_____

_____

_____

_____

_____

Choose your next adventure: turn the page for the simple stick, or go to page 129 for a *not a stick*.

The Stick: An Oldie But a Goodie

A 2008 inductee into the National Toy Hall of Fame, the stick is one of the oldest and most played-with toys in human history. Stick play offers children the opportunity to *practice* being careful, to *practice* assessing danger, and to *practice* mindfulness. It also engages imaginations: a stick is as open ended and as flexible a manipulative as a cardboard box is. You can write with it in sand, stick it into the ground to build a tent, use it to make real or imaginary fires, poke things with it, use it in symbolic play, and so much more.

Process

1. Acquire sticks.
2. Develop a basic stick play policy. In Jeff's program, the stick play policy is *Be Careful*. He offers the kids reminders and suggestions as needed about what *careful* looks like. Those who have trouble doing *careful* stick play lose their stick play privileges for the day.
3. Let the play commence.

Ingredients

❑ Sticks—thick sticks and thin sticks, long sticks and short sticks, sticks with bark and sticks without, fresh sticks that are still bendy and green inside, and well-aged sticks that are dry and brittle.

A Bit of Danger Is Okay

Sticks are potentially dangerous—but *everything* is *potentially* dangerous. *Everything* could kill you, *everything* could be risky, *everything* could be toxic. If you grow up believing you cannot safely walk across a yard while carrying a stick, or ride in a grocery cart without buckling the seat belt, or jump from a retaining wall without breaking your leg, you grow up with limited experience in assessing real danger. Kids who grow up protected from so many *potential* dangers have a hard time shaking the idea that the world is out to get them. They become fearful of new situations and experiences.

We suppose it is possible to pass through childhood without playing with sticks and come out on the other side a fully functioning and happy adult—but we don't recommend it.

More Play Adventures

- *Inside stick play*. Craft sticks, chopsticks, bamboo skewers, toothpicks, and drinking straws make good sticks for inside play.
- *Beat it*. Get your rhythm on with drumsticks and rhythm sticks.
- *Go old school*. Lincoln Logs, pick-up sticks, and Tinkertoys are great old-school, stick-based toys that the kids will enjoy.

Stick-Based Toys

After Jeff's books *Do-It-Yourself Early Learning* and *Everyday Early Learning* came out, people who didn't want to do it themselves suggested he start making toys that they could buy from him. After hearing this a few dozen times, he decided to give it a try. Over the years, he has developed a lot of stick-based toys using reclaimed urban wood. You can check them out at explorationsearlylearning.com/shop.

- *Sticks at mealtime.* Grill some chicken or turkey drumsticks, cook food on kebab sticks, or slip hotdogs on the end of pointy sticks and cook them over a fire that you and the kids have made with sticks.
- *Build some people.* Make stick figures using real sticks—hold them together with rubber bands or duct tape.
- *Get physical.* For some great large-muscle play, hook kids up with pogo sticks or a pair of stilts.

Related Books and Songs

- *Not a Stick* by Antoinette Portis
- *Cooking on a Stick: Campfire Recipes for Kids* by Linda White
- *Stick Kid* by Peter Holwitz
- "Tap Your Sticks" by Music with Mar
- "Apple on a Stick," a hand-clapping song
- "And the Green Grass Grew All Around" by William Jerome and Harry Von Tilzer

Notes

_____

_____

_____

_____

_____

_____

_____

_____

Choose your next adventure: turn the page and make some thuds, or go to
page 137 and make some suds.

Packing Tape Drum

This adventure is our version of the packing tape drum made by Australian early learning music guru and play advocate Alec Duncan, and it's one of two activities in *Let's Play* inspired by Alec. Kids will enjoy both building drums and playing them. They will also learn about sound, social skills, problem solving, following directions, and more.

Process

1. Stretch a length of tape across an open end of the bucket. Make it as tight as possible, and make sure there are a few inches of tape down each side of the container. Run your hands over the tape down the side of the bucket to firmly secure the tape. Don't worry about ripples.

Ingredients

- ❑ Clear packing tape
- ❑ 5-gallon bucket
- ❑ Scissors
- ❑ Your own set of earplugs (*optional*)

2. Turn the bucket 90 degrees and repeat the previous step.

3. Next, rotate the bucket a few degrees and apply another crisscross of tape. Continue this process of rotating and taping until the entire surface of the bucket is covered with tape. Make sure there aren't any gaps in the tape and that each piece of tape is firmly secured to the bucket.

4. Now do it all over again: apply a second layer of tape over the first.

5. Last, turn the bucket over and press down on the sticky side of the tape against a hard, flat surface so the two layers stick to each other.

More Play Adventures

- *Make different sizes.* The size of your drum determines the sound of your drum. Try making them out of different sizes of PVC pipe connectors, assorted pails and buckets, and other objects.

- *Use different materials.* Any rigid container will work—baby formula cans, paint cans, 5-gallon buckets, an old car tire, or a 55-gallon drum. Flexible, bendy containers (think yogurt containers) will not work. If you end up using a container with a bottom, you might want to cut the bottom out or cut a hole or holes in the container's side. A hole allows the air pressure to equalize when the drum is struck. A hole isn't necessary, but the drum will sound better if there is one.

Drum Notes

Here are a few notes for successful drum play:

- Your packing tape drum skin will not last forever. Wear and tear will take its toll, and after a few weeks of regular use, you will probably have to spend a few minutes replacing it. This is not because the kids are being too rough. It's because tape that gets beat on a lot wears out.
- If you work with more than one child, make more than one drum.
- Plan on noise. We were only half joking when we added earplugs to the Ingredients list. This is a better *outside-during-a-warm-summer-day* toy than it is an *inside-because-it-is-raining-while-the-baby-is-sleeping* toy.

About Alec

While working in child care, Alec started building instruments from recycled materials for kids to play with. Since then, he has built up a following on Facebook and YouTube, where he advocates for music in early learning settings as well as child-led, play-based learning. You can learn more about Alec's work and connect with him by visiting his website (childsplaymusic.com.au), his YouTube channel (www.youtube.com/user/childplaymusic), or his Facebook page (www.facebook.com/ChildsPlayMusicPerth).

- *Decorate your drum.* Make your drum pretty by letting the kids decorate its body with markers, paint, glitter, and so on, before you add the packing-tape skin.
- *Make drumsticks.* Half-inch wooden dowels, chopsticks, wooden spoons, 10- to 12-inch sections of garden hose, old flip-flops—all these things will work as drumsticks and produce different sounds when they strike the drum.

Related Books and Songs

- *To Be a Drum* by Evelyn Coleman
- *Drum City* by Thea Guidone
- *Jungle Drum* by Deanna Wundrow
- *Jungle Drums* by Graeme Base
- *All about Drums* by Greg Roza
- "Drum Boogie" by Gene Krupa
- "Tribal Drums" by Tribe: Native American Drums and Flute Music
- "African Dance Drums" by African Drums

Notes

_____

_____

_____

_____

_____

_____

_____

_____

Choose your next adventure: turn the page for water and sound, or go to page 108, where eggs hit the ground.

Water Play Sounds

This adventure about creating sounds and music during water play was inspired by a blog post by Alec Duncan. (You can check out the blog post at http://childs playmusic.com.au/2012/01/17/water-play-music-play-children-a-natural-combination.) At its core, Water Play Sounds is about encouraging children to pay attention to different sounds. But it's also a great way to hone small-muscle skills, practice social skills and thinking skills, and learn a bit about how the physical world works. (Check out chapter 14 for ways to connect with Alec Duncan online.)

Process

1. Let the children play with the cups or bottles in the water. Just let them play and explore for a while.

2. Point out the sounds you hear. Encourage kids to listen to the sounds they create.

3. Ask them to conduct experiments to see how many different sounds they can make with the containers and water. Help them predict what sound specific actions will make.

4. Encourage them to listen carefully and introduce some descriptive vocabulary: *loud*, *quiet*, *soft*, *hard*, *drip*, *drop*, *splish*, *splash*, *tinkle*, *sprinkle*, *swoosh*.

5. Try some of the variations below.

Ingredients

❑ Water play table, plastic tote, or wading pool
❑ Water
❑ Plastic cups or bottles

More Play Adventures

- *Metal bowls.* Float a few metal bowls on the water's surface. Tap them with wooden spoons. Tap them lightly and then tap them hard. Tap quickly and slowly. Add some water to the bowls and tap some more. Add or remove water and tap again. Talk about how the sounds change.

- *Metal lid.* Hold a metal pot lid partly in the water and tap it with a wooden spoon. Submerge it to different depths and listen to how the sound changes. Tap it when it's out of the water and then submerge one side while it's still vibrating. You can also try tapping metal spoons or sticks on the metal lid, and then replace the metal lid with a pizza pan or a cookie sheet.

- *Corrugated plastic pipe.* Submerge one end of a short piece of corrugated pipe and then run a wooden spoon or stick across the pipe's ridges. Vary how deeply the pipe is submerged as well as the speed of the spoon to change the sound.

- *Turkey basters.* Listen to the sound water makes when it is squirted from a turkey baster. Squirt the water onto different surfaces: bowls, cookie sheets, plastic water bottles, skin, and so on.
- *Plastic tubing.* Submerge the ends of sections of tubing into the water and have children blow into the other ends to make bubbles. Use clear drinking straws if you do not have plastic tubing. Pay attention to the sounds the bubbles make.
- *Golf balls.* Drop golf balls into the water and listen to the sounds they make. Drop them from an inch or so above the water's surface, and then drop them from as high as you can reach. How does the sound change? Next, try dropping stones of different sizes, ping-pong balls, metal washers, and other such items, and then talk about the sounds you hear.
- *Spray bottles.* Fill spray bottles with water. Then let the kids listen to the sounds they create when they spray water into the water play table (or plastic tote or wading pool). Experiment. How does it sound when they spray other things, like the ground, cookie sheets, a bowl, dry paper towels, or plastic cups?

Related Books and Songs

- *Sounds All Around* by Wendy Pfeffer
- *Sound: Loud, Soft, High, and Low* by Natalie M. Rosinsky
- *Polar Bear, Polar Bear, What Do You Hear?* by Bill Martin Jr.
- *Sound Waves* by Ian F. Mahaney
- *What Is Sound?* by Charlotte Guillain
- "Drip, Drip, Drip" by Beethoven's Wig
- "Splish Splash" by Bobby Darin
- "Splash'n Twist" by Splash'n Boots

Notes

Choose your next adventure: turn the page for fun that blows through a hose, or go to page 15 for some critters without toes.

The Awesome Vacuum of Play

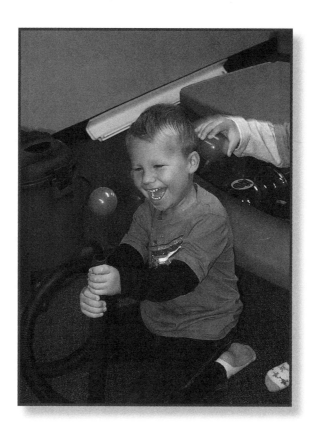

You probably have a shop vacuum in your basement or garage. If you don't, you probably know someone who has one you could borrow. Put this book down and go get it now, and then come back and finish reading this chapter. There's playing to do! You'll be amazed when you see how much fun and how much learning playing with a vacuum offers. For example, vacuum play can build visual-tracking skills, social skills, and problem-solving skills, as well as an understanding of cause-and-effect relationships. (*Note:* Clean out your vacuum and maybe change the filter before beginning the play.)

Process

1. Dump ping-pong balls on the ground.
2. Let the kids take turns sucking them up with the vacuum.
3. Remove the ping-pong balls from the vacuum.
4. Repeat.

Ingredients

- ❑ Shop vacuum (A 10-gallon wet/dry vac with a 5-horsepower motor and reversible airflow will work best.)
- ❑ Ping-pong balls

More Play Adventures

- *Try different materials.* Instead of ping-pong balls, try shredded paper, paper clips, packing peanuts, plastic beads, dry pasta, cereal, toothpicks, or Legos.
- *Exhale . . .* Reverse the flow of air on your vacuum by attaching the hose to the air output instead of the air intake. Then drop the ping-pong balls (or whatever material you're using) into the hose and turn the machine on. The balls will shoot from the hose and fly across the room. (*Note:* Some materials work better than others. For instance, bits of yarn work better than rocks.)
- *Get messy.* Invite children to pour flour, instant oatmeal, instant grits, or confetti down the vacuum hose. Make sure the machine is set to air output, let the kids take turns aiming it, and turn it on. Be prepared for a great big mess.
- *Get wet.* With the vacuum turned on and blowing out air, invite the children to slowly pour water into the end of the hose. The water will turn to a fine mist and fly into the air. Alternatively, let them pour water down into the hose before turning the vacuum on and see what happens. Let the children experiment with the effects different amounts of water create. Everyone will have a fun, *wet* time.

Jeff's Awesome Vacuum of Play

Jeff blinged out his vacuum by painting the canister with chrome spray paint, sticking on silver skull decals, and attaching red LED lights turned on by a button he installed. Jeff's vacuum has traveled with him to training events all over the country, and kids and adults love playing with it. You might say they're having good clean fun.

Noisy Stuff

The noise of the vacuum may be overwhelming to some kids. Invest in some inexpensive earplugs (we recommend over-the-ear versions) so sound-sensitive kids can play in comfort.

- *Inhale some bubbles.* Set the vacuum to air intake. Have some of the kids make bubbles with bubble soap, bubble wands, and their own breath. Have the rest of the kids take turns using the vacuum to suck the floating soap bubbles out of the air.
- *Let the TP fly.* Place a roll of toilet paper (use the cheap stuff) on a stick. Make sure the end of the paper is loose so it will unwind. Invite the children to hold the stick in front of the vacuum hose (set to air output), let them turn on the machine, and watch what happens. Then let the children experiment to find the right hose-to-stick position to speed up the unwinding. Once they do, they can unwind the whole roll in no time flat. Time them with a stopwatch or cell phone timer. (Jeff's record is about thirteen seconds for a roll of two-ply.) Once you're done, you can reverse the airflow and suck up the paper.

- *Up, up in the air.* Inflate some balloons and let the kids use the vacuum to blow them up in the air. How many balloons can they keep aloft at once? For how long can they keep the balloon aloft?
- *Bring on the bling.* Let's face it: shop vacuums aren't much to look at. If you're lucky enough to have your own, we suggest you let the kids pretty it up a bit. Spray paint it, stencil it, bedazzle it, add LED lighting, and stick decals or stickers on it. Do something to make it look good.

Related Books and Songs

- *Engelbert Sneem and His Dream Vacuum Machine* by Daniel Postgate
- *Vacuum Cleaners* by Elaine Marie Alphin
- *Rhyming Dust Bunnies* by Jan Thomas
- *The Day Jake Vacuumed* by Simon James
- "Vacuum Cleaner Hoses" by Willio & Phillio
- "Vickie the Vacuum" by Candy and the Sweet Tooths

Notes

_____

_____

_____

_____

_____

_____

_____

_____

Choose your next adventure: turn the page and build a fantastic frame, or go to page 121 for a project that has met with fan-tastic acclaim.

Play Frame

The Play Frame is a PVC structure you can use for all kinds of play—pulley play, water play, pendulum play, art, weaving, and more. It's a versatile piece of equipment, so you'll get a lot of use out of it.

Process

1. Cut the first piece of PVC pipe in half to create two 60-inch pieces.
2. Cut the second piece of PVC pipe into a 60-inch piece and four 15-inch pieces.
3. Attach the elbows to the ends of a 60-inch piece of pipe. Do not glue anything yet. Make sure the pieces all fit together nicely first.

4. Connect a 15-inch piece of pipe to the opposite ends of each T fitting.

5. Finish the uprights by connecting the remaining 60-inch pieces to the third hole in each T.

6. Attach the uprights to the open holes in the elbows.

7. With the frame firmly assembled, drill a hole perpendicular to the ground down through the center of the crosspiece.

8. Put a washer on the eyehook and thread it from the bottom through the hole you just drilled.

9. Add the second washer to the threaded top of the eyehook, and use an adjustable wrench to secure it in place with the locking nut.

10. If everything looks right, glue all the pieces into place, following the instructions included with the PVC cement. If it looks nothing like the frame in the photos, take it apart and start over.

11. Now it's time for play. Use your Play Frame and the variations below to support some play.

Ingredients

- ❏ Two 10-foot pieces of 2-inch Schedule 40 PVC
- ❏ Two 2-inch Schedule 40 PVC elbows
- ❏ Two 2-inch Schedule 40 PVC T fittings
- ❏ Eyehook, 1/4-inch diameter and 4 inches long
- ❏ Two 1/4-inch washers
- ❏ One 1/4-inch locking nut
- ❏ Something to cut the PVC with (A handsaw or electric chop saw will do the job.)
- ❏ Drill with a 1/4-inch bit
- ❏ Adjustable wrench
- ❏ PVC primer and glue (*optional*)

More Play Adventures

- *Pulley play.* Hang a pulley from the eyehook in your Play Frame, thread some rope through the pulley, tie a bucket to one end of the rope, and let the kids play. For best results, add some sandbags or other weights to the feet of the Play Frame to steady it.

- *Pendulum play.* Use duct tape to secure a thin piece of rope to a plastic bottle full of sand or water. Thread the other end of the rope through the eyehook in the Play Frame, and tie it off so the bottle dangles a few inches from the ground. Now let the kids swing the pendulum and knock things over. Small cardboard boxes and oatmeal containers work great.

- *Marble roll.* You can use your Play Frame to support the Pool Noodle Raceway from chapter 9 (page 39).

- *Tape play.* Grab a few rolls of masking tape and let the kids create a spider web on the Play Frame. Then let them stick things to the web.

- *Easel construction.* Cut a piece of 1/4-inch hard-board or plywood about 48 x 40 inches. Next, drill a 1/2-inch hole in each corner and halfway along each edge. Take some bungee cords or rope, and use the holes to suspend the panel in the frame. Now you can tape paper to both sides of the panel and kids can draw, color, or paint.
- *Weaving fun.* Tie the end of a skein of yarn to an upper corner of the play frame and wrap the yarn horizontally around both frame uprights, leaving about an inch of space between each pass, until you reach the bottom of the frame. Tie off the yarn. To keep it in place, run a strip of duct tape up both of the frame's uprights. Now let the kids weave things into the yarn: long blades of grass, sticks, pool noodles, pipe cleaners, flagging tape, strips of fabric.
- *Water play.* To use the play frame for water play, you'll need some more equipment from the plumbing and automotive departments of your local home improvement store. Just follow the instructions below.

Process

1. Snip the tube into 12- to 36-inch pieces.
2. Attach the bungee cords horizontally across the Play Frame so the children will have someplace to attach the tubes and fittings. Provide masking tape so they can secure the tubes to the cords and Play Frame.
3. Put out the materials and let the children start to connect the pieces, add funnels, and attach ball valves.
4. Make water available, and when the kids are ready, they'll start pouring it into the funnels. As play progresses, ask some challenge questions, such as: Is the water flowing through all of the tubes? Can they build something that will mix two different colors of water? How about mixing three, four, or more colors?

Ingredients

- ❏ 1/2-inch barbed fittings—go with plastic drip irrigation fittings or brass PEX fittings.
- ❏ 4 or more T fittings, elbows, and straight connectors
- ❏ 10 feet or more of clear plastic tubing with an inside diameter of 5/8 inch
- ❏ 2 or 3 1/2-inch barbed ball valves—these will get you started.
- ❏ 2 or 3 funnels that fit snugly into the end of the tubing
- ❏ 6 bungee cords (or masking tape)

Tabletop Play Frame. Want something smaller for tabletop play? Follow these instructions and you will end up with a smaller version of the Play Frame in the photos that will be perfect for tabletop play:

Process

1. From the first piece of PVC pipe, cut three 36-inch pieces.
2. From the second piece of PVC pipe, cut four 10-inch pieces.
3. Attach an elbow to the ends of a 36-inch piece of pipe. (Do not glue anything yet—make sure the pieces all fit together nicely first.)
4. Connect a 10-inch piece of pipe to the opposite ends of each T fitting.
5. Finish the uprights by connecting the remaining 36-inch pieces to the third hole in each T.

Ingredients

- ❑ Two 10-foot pieces of 1-inch Schedule 40 PVC
- ❑ Two 1-inch Schedule 40 PVC elbows
- ❑ Two 1-inch Schedule 40 PVC T fittings
- ❑ Eyehook, 1/4-inch diameter and 2 inches long
- ❑ Two 1/4-inch washers
- ❑ One 1/4-inch locking nut
- ❑ Something to cut the PVC with (A handsaw or electric chop saw will do the job.)
- ❑ Drill with a 1/4-inch bit
- ❑ Adjustable wrench
- ❑ PVC primer and glue (*optional*)

6. Attach the uprights to the open holes in the elbows.
7. With the frame firmly assembled, drill a hole perpendicular to the ground down through the center of the crosspiece.
8. Put a washer on the eyehook and thread it from the bottom through the hole you just drilled.
9. Add the second washer to the threaded top of the eyehook, and use an adjustable wrench to secure it in place with the locking nut.
10. Now, if everything looks right, you can glue all the pieces into place following the instructions on your PVC primer and cement. If it does not look like a small version of the frame in the photos, take it apart and start over. Use the tabletop frame in all the ways

the large one is used above. For an easel, cut your hardboard or plywood into a 30- x 20-inch rectangle.

Related Books and Songs

- *Forces Make Things Move* by Kimberly Brubaker Bradley
- *Motion: Push and Pull, Fast and Slow* by Darlene R. Stille
- *Pull, Lift, and Lower: A Book about Pulleys* by Michael Dahl
- *What Is a Pulley?* by Lloyd G. Douglas
- *Wild Rose's Weaving* by Ginger Churchill
- "Let the Pendulum Swing" by Julia Loggins and Steve Wood
- "Swing Low Sweet Chariot" by Bill Schaeffer

Notes

_____

_____

_____

_____

_____

_____

_____

_____

Choose your next adventure: see the next page and flex your imagination, or go to page 149 for a hydration and irrigation innovation.

The Empty Box: The Ultimate Imagination Inspiration

Most modern toys have *too* many batteries, *too* much plastic, *too* many marketing tie-ins, and *not* enough flexibility. It's important for adults to remember that play, imagination, and creativity flow from children—not from toys. A good toy is an open-ended one, a blank slate with which children can create, imagine, and endlessly play. In this adventure, the blank slate is a cardboard box—a bunch of them, in fact. Empty boxes provide kids with a chance to flex their imaginations, think up solutions to problems, and conjure new ideas. When you offer this project, be ready to shoot some video or take pictures. You'll want to capture what happens.

1. Collect a bunch of boxes. (Have the children's families bring in boxes for a month or so leading up to your empty box adventure.)

2. If you can, remove all the toys from your space so the boxes get plenty of room and the full attention of the kids. You can add toys and other materials into the environment when the kids request them: "I need some baby dolls for the hospital we built," "Can I have markers to decorate the boxes?" "We need scissors to cut some windows."

3. Add a lot of boxes. Seventy-five is not too many. Tape some of them so that one end is open, tape others so that both ends are open, tape still others so that both ends are closed, and leave some of them flattened.

4. Step back, observe, and enjoy the boundless imaginations of young children.

Ingredients

- ❑ Small empty boxes
- ❑ Medium empty boxes
- ❑ Large empty boxes
- ❑ Packing tape
- ❑ Lots of time
- ❑ Lots of space

Denita's Box Experiment

After a month of collecting boxes of all shapes and sizes from the children's families, I was prepared for the Empty Box Experiment. Except for the dolls, cars, and balls, I removed all the toys from my child care space (these days, I'd remove all the toys, including the dolls, cars, and balls, and let the kids request them to practice asking for what they need) and then filled the room with seventy-five assorted boxes.

The result? Kids created minivans and train cars by climbing inside boxes with their ends taped open, lifting them up, and walking along. A large HDTV box with a slippery label became an ice skating rink when we flattened it and laid it on the floor. Taped-shut boxes were used to create kitchens, towers, beds, castles, caves, machines, spaceships, robots, and more. The children's imaginations and creativity bloomed, and two years later, their favorite toys are still the various empty boxes we keep in the playroom.

More Play Adventures

- *Add some open-ended props.* To keep the box play going, add things like empty peanut butter jars, baby dolls, wooden blocks, blankets, or toy cars.
- *Add tape.* Cardboard boxes and tape go together like ice cream and chocolate syrup. Masking tape is easier for kids to use on their own; duct tape and packing tape stick better, but they are more challenging for kids to work with.
- *Create some panels.* Take three identical flattened boxes and duct-tape them together end-to-end, creating a long panel. Make sure to tape them so they can be folded—you want a flexible joint where the boxes meet. These panels can be used for making everything from fences to walls, from forts to Skee-Ball games, from bridges to sandy beaches.
- *Bring it outside.* Don't have the time or ambition to move all your toys out of the playroom? How about creating an outdoors cardboard box wonderland instead? Just follow the process already described in your outdoor play area.

- *Water play.* While you're outside, why not get the hose out and do some cardboard box water play? Let the kids fill boxes with water, spray big boxes while their buddies hide inside them, or try to build water slides.
- *Decorate.* Get out the markers, crayons, and paint, and pretty up your boxes.
- *A cut above the rest.* How about using scissors or knives for cutting windows and doors into boxes? This may sound dangerous, but with proper supervision and help, children ages three and up are capable of it—and trusting them with these tools will do a lot to build their self-esteem and confidence.

Related Books and Songs

- *Not a Box* by Antoinette Portis
- *Look What You Can Make with Boxes: Creative Crafts from Everyday Objects* edited by Lorianne Siomades
- *The Box* by Kevin O'Malley

- *Henry's Freedom Box: A True Story from the Underground Railroad* by Ellen Levine
- *The Birthday Box* by Leslie Patricelli
- "The Cardboard Box" by Ronnie Mackie
- "Cardboard Wings" by Ish

Notes

_____

_____

_____

_____

_____

_____

_____

Choose your next adventure: see the next page for play magnetic, or go to page 39 for play quite kinetic.

Flex Magnets

Children will have a ton of fun with these flexible magnet toys. They can manipulate them into interesting tabletop sculptures, stick them to the refrigerator, make jewelry, and more. Flex Magnets really are a new twist on magnet play that, among other things, builds pre-writing skills like small-muscle control, hand-eye coordination, visual tracking, and the ability to differentiate between positive and negative space.

Process

1. Braid three pipe cleaners together.
2. Hot-glue a magnet to each of the braided ends of the pipe cleaners.
3. Let the glue dry completely.
4. Let the children play.

Ingredients
(yields ten Flex Magnets)

❑ 20 1- x 1/8-inch ceramic disc magnets
❑ 30 pipe cleaners
❑ Hot glue gun

Note: Trust kids as capable learners and get them involved in the braiding and glue gun work as much as possible.

More Play Adventures

Get the kids involved in making some of the magnet toys described below, and then let them lead their play and learning, by allowing them to figure out where, and how, and what to play.

- *More magnets.* Glue a third magnet to the middle of your braided pipe cleaners.
- *Different materials.* You can use magnetic hematite, 14 gauge electrical wire, and duct tape instead of the materials listed above. Just cut 10- to 12-inch sections of wire and use narrow strips of colored duct tape to secure a magnet to each end. (Glue does not work too well on the hematite because it's so smooth.)

- *Magnetic bandana.* Take a bandana, place a magnet in one corner, fold the corner over to cover the magnet, and then sew it in place so the bandana has a magnetized corner. Then just repeat for the other three corners.
- *Go big.* Use larger ceramic magnets and connect them with 24-inch lengths of 12 gauge wire.
- *No bend.* Instead of pipe cleaners, connect the magnets to a chopstick using hot glue.

Related Books and Songs

- *What Makes a Magnet?* by Franklyn M. Branley
- *Magnets: Pulling Together, Pushing Apart* by Natalie M. Rosinsky
- *Janice VanCleave's Magnets: Mind-boggling Experiments You Can Turn into Science Fair Projects* by Janice VanCleave
- *A Look at Magnets* by Barbara Alpert
- "Magnets" by Music with Mar
- "You Spin Me Round (Like a Record)" by Dead or Alive
- "Opposites Attract" by Paula Abdul

Notes

_____

_____

_____

_____

_____

_____

_____

Choose your next adventure: turn the page and head for attempts at breaking, or go to page 132 for some mess making.

Don't Break the Bed!

If you have a copy of *The Napping House* by Audrey Wood, or you can borrow a copy from the library, read it to the children. *The Napping House* was, in fact, the inspiration for this activity and is the perfect way to introduce it. The goal of "Don't Break the Bed" is to get the kids to experiment with different materials in order to discover their breaking points. But you don't have to read the book to get started. You can initiate the activity when someone's sheet of paper rips during a craft project, or when someone's bridge or building falls during block play. Or you could just say, "Hey, how much stuff could we pile on this sheet of wrapping paper before it breaks?" Once you get the "Let's see what it takes to break this stuff" idea into their heads, the rest is easy. The learning also flows. As they experiment, kids build problem-solving skills, hone cause-and-effect thinking skills, practice social skills, and build small- and large-muscle skills.

1. Select two children to be holders—one for each end of the material you've decided to test.

2. Let the rest of the children take turns adding items to the material, aka the bed. It's best if you give the children a chance to organize the turn-taking process themselves. There is a good chance they'll be more successful at waiting their turn when they have ownership of the process. Remember, the way kids learn to be patient and to take turns is by practicing.

Ingredients

- ❑ A variety of bed materials: plastic wrap, aluminum foil, wrapping paper, toilet paper, paper towels, newspaper, tissue paper, wrapping paper, butcher paper
- ❑ Toys of various sizes
- ❑ Time to experiment

3. When the first bed breaks, do the test again. Use the same material for the bed, or try a different one. Stack the same stuff on the bed, or stack different stuff. And give the kids as much control as they can handle in choosing the new holders for each test.

4. Repeat until the children are bored, hungry, need a nap, or have to go home.

From Story to Spark

This activity was originally sparked while Denita presented a literacy skills workshop in Sioux City, Iowa. She was talking about *The Napping House* by Audrey Wood. In the story, grandma is enjoying a lovely nap on a cozy, rainy afternoon. Her grandson, a dog, a cat, a mouse, and finally a flea soon join her. Each lies down on top of the last one. In the end, the bed breaks, and the tower of napping people and critters are no longer sleeping.

Fast-forward to Denita's family child care program a month or two later. It was a rainy day, and the group was reading *The Napping House*. When they finished, Denita asked, "What could we roll out and hold onto to make the bed?"

It didn't take long before little Mallory had an idea. "Nita! We could use toilet paper to make a bed. Toilet paper would break." The kids acted out the story, piling on different toys until the toilet paper bed broke.

And so began a morning full of sharing, taking turns, and experimenting while many beds made of many different materials—aluminum foil, plastic wrap, paper towel, and toilet paper—were tested. (The plastic wrap bed never did break!) Most important, the children felt empowered as they tested their own ideas and learned through trial and error.

- *Keep records.* If you like, you can select someone (or a couple someones) to keep records. Provide a clipboard (there is something so special about being the one to hold the clipboard), paper, and pen, and show the record keeper(s) how to keep track of the number of items it takes to break the bed.

- *Have more holders.* Go with four or more holders if you have a large bed to test or a lot of busy brains to keep busy. Note that the number of holders can impact the amount of weight the material can hold as well as how long it takes to break.

- *Use some probably-won't-break materials.* Test materials like bed sheets, blankets, plastic drop cloths, parachutes, pieces of wood, or plastic rain gutters. (See more rain gutter activities in chapter 36, page 149.) The goal here will not be to see how much stuff the bed can hold before breaking but how much the *holders* can *hold*.

- *Just add water.* See how much water a bed made from plastic wrap can hold. How about a paper towel bed? Does the water behave differently with different

materials? How about going bigger and trying water on a piece of plastic drop cloth or a bed sheet? Can you add water to the bed sheet fast enough for a puddle to form?

- *Ice it.* Try adding ice to the different materials. What will happen if you add ice cubes to a paper towel bed? How much ice does it take to break an aluminum foil bed? You can bring some variety to this play adventure by preparing different sized ice cubes ahead of time. While you're at it, you might as well use liquid watercolor to make colored ice, or freeze small objects into the cubes—or both.

- *Build a water tower.* Suspend a long board (or plastic rain gutter) between two chairs so it's a few feet off the ground. Now let the kids experiment with filling cups with water and then stacking them on the board to create a tower. How tall a tower can they build before the structure falls? Now pick up the cups and start again.

- *Stack 'em biggest to smallest.* Use the toys in your playroom as blocks and build a tower, going from biggest toys on the bottom to smallest on top. If the tower doesn't break on its own, help it out so everyone can enjoy the crash.

Related Books and Songs

- *The Napping House* by Audrey Wood
- *Bridges!: Amazing Structures to Design, Build & Test* by Carol A. Johmann, Elizabeth Rieth, and Michael P. Kline
- *London Bridge Is Falling Down!* by Peter Spier
- *The Fall of Freddie the Leaf: A Story of Life for All Ages* by Leo Buscaglia
- *No Jumping on the Bed!* by Tedd Arnold
- *Five Little Monkeys Jumping on the Bed* by Eileen Christelow
- *Nathaniel Willy, Scared Silly* by Judith Mathews and Fay Robinson
- "I Need a Nap" by Kate Winslet and "Weird Al" Yankovic
- "Broken Bed Blues" by the Space City Cowboys

Notes

_____

_____

_____

_____

_____

_____

_____

_____

Choose your next adventure: see the next page and grab it, or go to page 34 and paint it.

Grab It

Have you ever seen those grabber things at the home center or big box store? They're about 3 feet long with a pincer on one end, and they're used to pick up trash in the yard or reach cans of cat food on high shelves. If you practiced a little, we think you could even use them to change really ripe diapers. Anyway, get ahold of a few of these grabber things, because when put in the hands of a curious child, a lot of learning happens. They can help build hand-eye coordination, visual tracking and planning skills, and small- and large-muscle control. They can also inspire imaginations, improve problem-solving abilities, and create feelings of pride and accomplishment.

Process

1. Plop the grabbers on the floor with a few containers and some objects that can be grabbed.

2. Step back and observe. Do not demonstrate how to use the grabbers. If a child misuses one, step in and nudge her toward appropriate behavior by saying something like, "Mindy, these things are not swords. Can you figure out something to do with them besides stabbing your brother?"

More Play Adventures

- *Hang and grab.* Attach some lightweight items to pieces of yarn and then tape the yarn to your ceiling. Let the kids grab the items and pull them down with the grabbers. You can tape the yarn to tree branches and let the children pull items down outside. Denita used her Mystery Word letters (see chapter 1, page 1), and the kids ended up building words with them.

- *Rescue something.* Hide stuffed animals in a tree around a bunch of kids with access to grabbers, and you've created motivation to rescue the animals! Let the children problem solve. They may ask to use ladders or chairs.

Ingredients

❑ Grabbers (aka Easy Reach Tool, Grabber Tool, Trash Grabber)

❑ Small objects for grabbing: fluffy pom-poms, small foam blocks, scrunched-up pieces of paper, yarn pieces, coiled-up pipe cleaners, aluminum foil balls, mesh bath sponges, wooden blocks, and the like

❑ Containers for sorting: buckets, plastic totes, cardboard boxes

Create Some Scarcity

We're big advocates for going big and giving kids all the materials and supplies they need, but once in a while, we don't have enough grabbers, or tape, or funnels for everyone. Have more than one, but don't have so many that each child has one. Children need opportunities to practice dealing with scarcity. Scarcity helps them practice taking turns and sharing. It helps them practice selflessness, patience, and empathy. Thoughtfully creating scarcity with the grabbers or any other material provides children with a chance to practice these skills.

Denita's First Grabber Experience

The first time I introduced the grabbers, I simply plopped them on the floor with an assortment of small foam blocks and four empty buckets. I didn't demonstrate the grabbers—I just plopped them.

Questions and conversation started flying: "WHOA! What are these?" "Guys! I think I know. Look what it does!" "Watch me!" "Oh! I see! I can do that too!" "Wow, this is hard work!" "Look! I picked up a red one!" "Cool! They can grab stuff far away!" "Look out!! I have a green one, and the green ones are monsters!" Eventually, the kids joined forces, picked up every single block, and sorted them by color into different buckets. Then, using the grabbers, they worked together to overturn the buckets and dump the contents back onto the floor. The kids were very proud that they accomplished this task without ever touching the buckets with their hands. And I knew from this first experience that the grabbers had a lot of potential for fun, play, and learning.

- *Play messy.* Using grabbers during any messy play activity makes the activity fresh—and possibly even more messy. As an example, you could place grab-able objects in a tote full of mud or shaving cream and have the kids pluck them out with the grabbers.
- *Get creative.* Let kids try to color or paint using the grabbers.
- *Don't break the bed.* Do the Don't Break the Bed activity (see chapter 20, page 82) and have the holders try using the grabbers to hold the material instead of their hands.

Related Books and Songs

- *Cranes (Mighty Machines)* by Amanda Askew
- *Guess Who Grabs* by Sharon Gordon
- *Machines at Work* by Byron Barton
- *Moving Heavy Things* by Jan Adkins
- "Squish Me Squeeze Me (Live)" by Brady Rymer and the Little Band That Could
- "Baby Angst (Everybody Wants to Pinch My Cheeks!)" by Silly Joe
- "Squeeze Box" by the Who

_____

_____

_____

_____

_____

_____

_____

_____

Choose your next adventure: see the next page and kids must be mighty, or go to page 112 and things get flighty.

Another Brick in the Yard

This is one of our favorite kinds of activities because it uses simple materials, requires little preparation, and leads to big child-led play. Brick play will help kids develop large- and small-muscle control, problem-solving skills, social skills, and creative-thinking skills. They will also hone their skills in kinesthetic awareness, risk assessment, and situational awareness. Kids will have so much fun toting, hauling, stacking, dumping, tumbling, clunking, tossing, flipping, knocking, and jiggering bricks that when it's time to go in for lunch, they'll yell across the play area, "Hey, teacher, leave us kids alone!"

Process

1. Pile the bricks someplace outside for kids to discover.
2. Let them play.

Ingredients

☐ Bricks or cement pavers, twenty or more of them. More is better.

More Play Adventures

- *Add stones.* Most communities have a sand and gravel company nearby that can provide stone for cheap. In our area, we can fill a pickup full of stone for less than thirty dollars. (It's probably twice that if you have the stone delivered.) Stones 6 to 8 inches in diameter are best.
- *Go for variety.* Most home centers have a vast variety of brick options. Add bricks of different sizes, colors, and shapes to your brick play area.
- *Build a wall.* Take the kids to look closely at some real brick walls to see how they are put together. How are the bricks arranged? How thick is the mortar? Then mix up some mortar of your own out of thick mud and use it to build a brick wall. Use cheap spatulas, wooden spoons, or sticks to spread the mud. Let it dry, and then let the kids knock it down.

It's Dangerous!

One of the complaints we've heard about this project was that it was DANGEROUS. Little Lenny *could* drop a brick on his foot. Glenn *could* scrape his knee on a brick. And Beatrice *could* pinch her precious little fingers. Those things *could* happen—and we think that's a good thing. Pinched fingers and scraped knees are good teachers. They help kids learn to be careful and to pay attention, and the only way to learn how to be careful and to pay attention is through real-life experiences. Kids learn to manage danger by encountering it in little doses, and that's what brick play offers. Dan, a three-year-old in Jeff's program, carelessly plopped a brick down on his index finger the first day he played with bricks. His face filled with surprise, he held his finger tightly with his other hand, he looked for blood, and then he said, "I'm not bleeding, but I'm still going to be more careful!"

- *Provide some planks.* We recommend that you use synthetic decking because it doesn't warp, splinter, or split.
- *Draw plans.* Encourage kids to draw up plans for things they want to build or to draw pictures of things they have already built.
- *Make your own bricks.* Collect some small plastic containers like the ones butter, sour cream, or yogurt come in, fill them with thick mud (you can mix in some straw to help the mud hold together), and let them dry. Then let the kids pop the dried mud bricks out of the containers and build with them.
- *Make a splash.* Dig a pit that's 12 inches deep and about 3 feet across and fill it with water. Then toss in some bricks and enjoy the splash. You can also toss the bricks into a tote or wading pool full of water, but the muddy pit is more fun and more memorable.
- *Decorate your bricks.* Use paint or sidewalk chalk, or simply paint the bricks with water.
- *Weigh them.* Grab a bathroom scale and see how many bricks it takes to equal the weight of a two-year-old, or how many bricks it takes to make the scale read *80*.
- *Topple them.* On a flat surface, stand the bricks up on end and topple them like dominos.

Related Books and Songs

- *The Three Pigs* by David Wiesner
- *The True Story of the Three Little Pigs* by Jon Scieszka
- *The Three Little Pigs: An Architectural Tale* by Steven Guarnaccia
- *The Three Little Wolves and the Big Bad Pig* by Eugene Trivizas
- "The Three Little Pigs" by Roald Dahl
- "Three Pigs Rap" by Music with Mar
- "Another Brick in the Wall" by Pink Floyd
- "Brick House" by The Commodores

_____

_____

_____

_____

_____

_____

_____

_____

Choose your next adventure: see the next page for a real soaking, or go to page 51 for textured rolling.

Absorbing
Play

New words can lead to exciting play, experimentation, and learning. Lots of big play happens when children crawl inside new words to see what they're all about. In the case of this adventure, the word is *absorbent*. It's not a really big or fancy word, but it's one that most young children haven't experienced much. (It's probably not in the working vocabulary of most kids.) And that makes it an ideal word to play with.

Process

1. Set out the supplies: sheets of paper towels, pipettes or droppers, and cups of colored water.
2. Drip a few drops of colored water onto the tabletop and then place a sheet of paper towel over it.
3. As the children look on, explain to them that the towel is *absorbing* the water. You

might say something like, "Oh, look! The paper towel is absorbing, or soaking up, the blue water really quickly."

4. Let them try *absorbing* with paper towels. Let the process evolve. This is a good time for you to be a quiet observer and enter the process only when it's absolutely necessary.

Ingredients

❑ Paper towels—the select-a-size ones work great for this activity
❑ Cups of colored water (we prefer liquid watercolor over food coloring)
❑ Pipettes or droppers

More Play Adventures

- *Spray away.* Instead of using pipettes, put out spray bottles filled with colored water. Obviously, self-regulation comes into play here. It can be tempting to spray a friend. But children need opportunities to practice self-control. Both regular spray bottles and handheld misters work great, and each provides a different small-motor challenge.

- *Sponge squeeze.* For a fun twist, exchange the paper towels for some sponges and a bucket for squeezing them after they have absorbed the water. Sponges make for a great small-muscle activity.

An Absorbing Experience

Denita poured water on the table and then said to the children who had gathered, "We have a mess! How are we going to fix it?" The answer came very quickly. "Get a paper towel!"

She obeyed, got the paper towel, and gave it to Ty, who placed it on the water. He lifted it up, and the water was gone. After Denita told the kids that the paper towel had absorbed the water, they wanted to do the experiment again and again, each time gaining more control and understanding of the process.

Eventually a child asked Denita to add color to the water, and soon the children were absorbing two different colors of water with one piece of paper towel, and then three different colors. The children used the words *absorb, absorbing, absorbed*, and even *absorbent* frequently throughout their play. Their vocabularies were enhanced in a hands-on sort of way—which is the best way possible!

- *Comparison fun.* Provide different materials and test their absorbency: diapers, baby wipes, paper towels, aluminum foil, stuffed animals, notepaper, sponges, cardboard, foam blocks—whatever you have on hand. After the kids have had some experience with *absorbing*, just plop the various items on the table, say something like, "Will these things absorb stuff?" and let them explore.
- *Different liquids.* This play adventure can quickly climb the messy scale, so be prepared. Try absorbing baby oil, cooking oil, shaving cream, Kool-Aid, mud, lotion, and any other gloppy, gloopy concoctions you can come up with.
- *More words.* Think about all the different words beyond *absorbent* you could use to introduce more of this sort of play, exploration, and learning. What could you do with words like *heavy, blow, crash, balance, bend, entwine, funnel, pendulum, evaporate, combine*, or *transparent*?

Related Books and Songs

- *Wet Dog!* by Elise Broach
- *A Drop of Water: A Book of Science and Wonder* by Walter Wick
- "All Wet" by Erin Lee & Marci
- "Dry Bones" by the Delta Rhythm Boys

Notes

_____

_____

_____

_____

_____

_____

_____

Choose your next adventure: see the next page and dots will make a shape, or go to page 157 for a project with duct tape.

Giant Connect the Dots

To recharge a child's environment with play and learning, all you have to do is change something: add something, move something, or take something away. Children are so observant that even the slightest change awakens their curiosity. For example, if you're four and you walk into a room with numbered circles taped to the floor, your curiosity grows and your brain starts asking questions: "*Why* are there circles on the floor?" "*Who* put the circles there?" "*What* are the circles for?" "*Why* do they have numbers?" Your brain then starts trying to answer those questions, using prior knowledge and the information it's collecting from the environment and from the other curious brains around you. This act of *trying to understand a change in the environment* results in play and in learning—including pre-numeracy skills, pre-literacy skills, social skills, and more. Now, on to the dots . . .

Process

1. Figure out what you want your dot-to-dot to represent. (We provide some possibilities in More Play Adventures on the next page, but please take this idea and run with it in any direction that works for you and your crew of kids.)

2. Cut some 4- to 6-inch circles from the paper.

3. Arrange the dots on the floor to make whatever shape you decided on.

4. Once you're happy with the placement, number the dots and tape them down.

5. When the children discover the circles and ask about them, respond with something simple like, "I don't know. What do *you* think they're for?"

6. Encourage the children to do some brainstorming about the dots. Ask for their ideas and validate each one. Toss around the pros and cons of each. If needed, offer some clues. Then, once the purpose of the dots has been determined—"We need to connect them"—solve the next problem: "How?"

7. Discuss ways to connect the circles and why they may or may not work ("A pencil is a good idea, but we're not supposed to write on the floor.") Try out some of the children's ideas, even if you know they won't work. Making mistakes is a great way to learn.

8. Once they settle on connecting the dots with yarn (they may need you to guide them in this direction), let the children take turns running the yarn from numbered dot to numbered dot. Tape the yarn to the dots with masking tape.

9. "What is it?" Once the dots are all connected, take some time to discuss what the children have created.

More Play Adventures

- *Hit the wall.* Try making your giant dot-to-dot on a wall instead of on the floor.
- *Take it outside.* Instead of circles, pound stakes into the ground, and let the kids connect them with brightly colored flagging tape.
- *Human dot-to-dot.* Instead of connecting the dots with yarn, have the kids get on the floor and connect the dots with their bodies. Stand up on a chair and get a picture of your human dot-to-dot.
- *Letter and number dot-to-dots.* Create dot-to-dots in the shape of letters or numbers.
- *Shape dot-to-dots.* Create triangle, circle, square, rectangle, and rhomboid dot-to-dots.

The Value of Mistakes

Children who are never given the opportunity to make mistakes—and to learn from them—are at a disadvantage. When they never make mistakes, children learn to fear them, and the fear of making mistakes kills curiosity, spontaneity, and effort. This fear leads children to give up trying new things. They begin thinking, "Why try? I could mess up, and that would be embarrassing."

Help children to value their mistakes and to realize the upside of getting it wrong now and then. Making mistakes often reveals the answers.

- *Book and song dot-to-dots.* Create dot-to-dots related to your favorite books or songs. For example, Denita introduced the book *The Mitten* by Jan Brett by putting on the floor a giant dot-to-dot of . . . you guessed it . . . a mitten! The dot-to-dot became part of the children's play as they chose to act out the story using the dot-to-dot mitten as a prop. Her crew would then pretend to be the various animals in the story (and characters of their own imaginations) and climb inside the mitten.
- *Kid-created dot-to-dots.* Once the kids are familiar with the dot-to-dot idea, let them make their own dot-to-dot. Give them control over the whole process—cutting the circles, numbering them, arranging them, taping them to the floor, and then connecting them.

Related Books and Songs

- *Dot* by Patricia Intriago
- *The Dot* by Peter H. Reynolds
- *Lots of Dots* by Craig Frazier
- *Press Here* by Hervé Tullet
- *Ten Black Dots* by Donald Crews
- *Follow the Line* by Laura Ljungkvist
- *Follow the Line to School* by Laura Ljungkvist
- "Yellow Polka Dot Bikini" by Bobby Vinton
- "Lines and Dots" by Lucky Diaz and the Family Jam Band
- "Connecting The Dots" by Bobs & Lolo

Notes

Choose your next adventure: turn the page for play dramatic, or go to page 62 for fun aquatic.

Dramatic Play 101

In some programs, dramatic play still manages to hang on for dear life. Unfortunately, it's typically so scripted, managed, and curtailed by the adults in charge that it hardly resembles the free, wide-open, imaginative play they experienced themselves in their own childhoods. (Denita, who grew up on the family farm, remembers dramatic play that involved fresh cow manure. Jeff remembers endless hours of dramatic play involving joyfully killing and decapitating his neighborhood buddies.) Dramatic play gives children a chance to practice for the adult world, work out social-emotional issues, face fears, seek challenges, build social skills, experiment, problem solve, and so much more. Try to restore to your program some old-school dramatic play—the kind of play that used to take place in basements, tree houses, backyards, and under the dining-room table.

Process

1. Provide the ingredients listed here.
2. Step off the stage.
3. Let them play.
4. Be available if your help is really needed—but try to give the children a chance to solve any problems that arise.

Ingredients

- ❑ Time—lots of it
- ❑ Space—lots of it
- ❑ Freedom—lots of it
- ❑ Trust—lots of it
- ❑ Props—some blocks, some dress-up clothes, some baby dolls, some cardboard boxes and cardboard tubes, some sticks (old-school dramatic play doesn't require a lot of props)

More Play Adventures

To keep dramatic play going, all you have to do is update the props to fit the children's interests:

- *Restaurant*. Provide a table, chairs, bowls, plates, spoons, menus, cups, and open-ended props like blocks or pinecones to serve as food.

Is It Really That Simple?

Usually it is. Given these few ingredients, most kids are able and ready to play. Some kids, on the other hand, are truly unable to initiate dramatic play because they've become so accustomed to having a well-intentioned adult script their time. These kids may need your help easing into independent dramatic play. Other children are so used to spending time in front of video screens that actual human-to-human interaction will be tough. You may need to provide these children with dramatic play scenarios, for instance, or take on a role in the play yourself, or stay extra close to the action to help out if a disagreement arises. Then, when the time is right, you can step back off the stage to give these children full ownership of their play.

- *Doctor.* Provide some dress-up clothes, some long Ace bandages, a box of Band-Aids, cardboard boxes to serve as medical machines, writing materials, and blankets.
- *Zoo.* Provide lots of toy animals and lots of cardboard boxes and blocks to make cages.

You get the idea. Follow the children's lead and provide them with open-ended props that fit their interests. The most important thing you can do is to let them own the play. That happens when you give them these simple things: time (lots of it), space (lots of it), freedom (lots of it), and trust (lots of it).

Related Books and Songs

- *Just Pretend! Creating Dramatic Play Centers with Young Children* by Judy Nyberg
- *Pretend* by Jennifer Plecas
- *Pretend You're a Cat* by Jean Marzollo
- "The Great Pretender" by The Platters
- "Let's Play Pretend" by Gina Minks
- "Pretend With Me" by Penelope Torribio

_____

_____

_____

_____

_____

_____

_____

Choose your next adventure: turn the page for something egg-citing, or go to page 6 for an activity that prepares little fingers for writing.

Humpty Dumpty Protective Gear

I n Denita's program, a child who'd just learned about the importance of *protective gear* (a sibling had worn protective gear while roller blading) made the comment that if Humpty Dumpty had been wearing protective gear, he wouldn't have needed anyone to put him back together again. *Spark!* Now the kids in Denita's program look forward to doing the Humpty Dumpty Protective Gear adventure every year. It's loads of fun and full of pre-numeracy learning, science learning, language learning, and social learning. We're betting the children in your program will enjoy it too.

1. Make some Humptys by letting the kids draw faces on the eggs. Set the Humptys aside.

2. Have the children brainstorm a list of materials they can use to create the protective gear. (You may have to suggest a few items to get the kids' ideas flowing.) Gather up all the protective-gear materials brainstormed by the kids.

3. Have each of the children wrap an egg in one of the materials, securing it with tape.

4. Once all the eggs have been wrapped up in protective gear, let the testing begin. Have each child take a turn getting a Humpty up the ladder or step stool. Then have her drop the Humpty onto the cookie sheet. Last, have her carefully unwrap the Humpty in front of the group.

5. Record the results. You could use a smiley face for an unscathed Humpty and a frown face for a broken Humpty. Make a point of discussing what was learned with each test, and point out that even protective gear that failed taught the group something about protecting Humpty.

6. Repeat the process until the eggs are gone or the kids are bored.

Ingredients

❑ Raw eggs (You read that correctly. Watching hardboiled eggs fall to their demise just isn't as much fun.)

❑ Various materials to make protective gear: paper towels, bubble wrap, diapers, toilet paper, elastic bandages (for instance, an Ace bandage), fabric scraps—*anything* you could possibly wrap an egg in

❑ Masking tape

❑ Ladder or step stool

❑ Large cookie sheet or jellyroll pan (for Humpty to fall onto)

❑ Clipboard, paper, and pen (to record the results)

Get Sciencey

You can introduce sciencey terms like *theory* and *variable* and *experiment* and *test* and *measure* and *validate*. Talk about how scientists must carefully measure and record results when performing tests, making sure all the variables are consistent when the test is repeated. Strive to make your Humpty protective gear trials as scientific as your group of young children can manage.

More Play Adventures

- *Humpty re-entry capsules.* You'll need some empty plastic containers with lids and various cushioning materials such as flour, crackers, cotton balls, Lego blocks, packing peanuts, sponges, water, and cereal. Let the children pack their Humpty into a container with whatever cushioning material they choose. Then they can drop their Humpty capsule from atop the ladder.
- *Crack eggs.* That's right. Buy a bunch of eggs, get out your largest bowl, and let the children crack away. (Worried? If everyone avoids licking raw eggs off their fingers and remembers to wash up afterward, then everything will be fine.)
- *Cook the cracked eggs.* Just pour the eggs into a skillet over low heat and let them slowly cook away. Allow the children to observe the eggs change from a slimy gunk into a beautiful white-with-yellow-polka-dots solid.
- *Try the slide.* Instead of dropping Humpty from a ladder in his protective gear, see if he can survive a trip down a slide.

- *Parachutes.* How about making parachutes for Humpty using fabric, plastic sheeting, string, yarn, and tape? Then drop him from a tall ladder or a balcony.
- *Build a wall.* Use blocks. How about using the bricks in chapter 22 (page 91)—to build a wall for Humpty to fall from? How high a wall can an unprotected Humpty fall from?
- *Go big.* How about trying goose eggs or even ostrich eggs? You can find them online by searching for *fresh goose eggs* or *fresh ostrich eggs*. They may be a bit pricey, but it would be an experience to remember.

Related Books and Songs

- *Humpty Dumpty* by Daniel Kirk
- *Who Pushed Humpty Dumpty? And Other Notorious Nursery Tale Mysteries* by David Levinthal
- *Humpty Dumpty Climbs Again* by Dave Horowitz
- *Dimity Dumpty: The Story of Humpty's Little Sister* by Bob Graham

- *The Egg* by M. P. Robertson
- *An Egg Is Quiet* by Dianna Aston
- "Crash Boom Bam!" by Meg Russell
- "Elephants Falling from the Sky" by Mr. Gee
- "Can't Help Falling in Love" by Elvis Presley

Notes

_____

_____

_____

_____

_____

_____

_____

_____

Choose your next adventure: turn the page for an activity that develops visual tracking, or go to page 91 and do some stacking.

Ready, Aim, Fire!

This activity is another example of how simple, everyday materials can lead to hours of play and learning. Plastic spoons—that's right, the kind that come with ice-cream sundaes and also in boxes of a hundred for only a few dollars—pack hours of projectile fun. Ready, Aim, Fire! is an excellent way to practice visual tracking skills, hone hand-eye coordination, practice problem solving, build small muscles, and learn about cause-and-effect relationships as well as trial and error.

Process

1. Choose a location for your catapult play. Indoors is okay if you're using fluffy projectiles, but you might want to go outside with the heavier, denser ammo.
2. Plop the spoons and the projectiles down in your selected play space.
3. Let the kids get ready, aim, and fire. (Just in case you were well-behaved in middle school: 1) Hold the lower part of the spoon handle firmly in one hand so the

spoon's bowl, the part you scoop up cereal with, faces up and away from you. 2) Use your thumb and first two fingers to grasp the top and the backside of the spoon's bowl and to hold the ammo in place. 3) Pull back on the spoon's bowl (and the ammo). 4) Aim. 5) Let go of the spoon's bowl and the ammo.)

4. Once the kids have had some practice randomly launching things, try some of the additional play adventures below.

More Play Adventures

- *Provide targets.* Drag out some buckets, totes, or cardboard boxes to serve as targets. See how far away the kids can stand while still hitting the target.
- *Splash down.* If you use a bucket or tote as a target, fill it with water. The ammo will make an awesome splash when it hits the target.
- *Try different spoons.* How about trying long-handled plastic spoons made for eating ice-cream sundaes or big-bowled plastic soup spoons?
- *Change the projectiles.* Any little object will work. Here are some examples we've had fun with: fluffy craft pom-poms, packing peanuts, cut-up pool noodles, Kix cereal, aluminum foil balls, scrunched-up pipe cleaners, small rocks, Barbie heads, pinecones, marbles, grapes, and balls of playdough. Messier ammo suggestions: Shaving cream, strawberry jam, grapes, or pudding. Fire these things at a wall so you get a good splat.

- *Launch water.* Use long-handled plastic measuring cups and catapult water.
- *Make some catchers.* Add some super-simple catchers to your play. First, cut the bottom 2 or 3 inches from a clean plastic milk jug and discard the bottom section. Use some duct tape to protect little fingers from the sharp plastic edge

on the remaining portion of the jug. (If you're planning on catching small items, make sure the jug lid is on.) Now some kids can launch and some can catch. These catchers also work great in water play or with the play sprinkler in chapter 10 (on page 44) because trying to catch water is awesome fun.

Related Books and Songs

- *The Art of the Catapult: Build Greek Ballistae, Roman Onagers, English Trebuchets, and More Ancient Artillery* by William Gurstelle
- *The Big Book of Catapult and Trebuchet Plans!* by Ron Toms
- *Stomp Rockets, Catapults, and Kaleidoscopes: 30+ Amazing Science Projects You Can Build for Less Than $1* by Curt Gabrielson
- *Catapult Design, Construction and Competition with the Projectile Throwing Engines of the Ancients* by Ron L. Toms, Dr. Bernard F. Barcio, and Sir Ralph Payne-Gallwey
- "Throw the Bean Bag" by Tessarose
- "Whip It" by Devo

Don't Have a Heart

Know those little candy Valentine conversational hearts ("B Mine", "I ♥ U")? Don't launch them inside. The hearts seemed like a good idea when Denita let the kids launch them: they were the right size, and they had enough weight to fly a decent distance. The problem was they made an annoying *ping* when they hit things; they hurt a bit when they struck flesh; and they were hard to find when cleanup time came. Choose your projectiles wisely.

_____

_____

_____

_____

_____

_____

_____

_____

Choose your next adventure: turn the page for playful abstraction, or go to page 99 for dot connection.

Squiggles

Offer a kid a Squiggle, and you offer him an open-ended play invitation. Squiggles are literally and figuratively flexible—they bend and twist into all kinds of play scenarios—and they're easy to find, easy to store, and inexpensive. "What's a Squiggle?" you ask.

It's a piece of yarn.

Simple materials often lead to big play. In this case, that play could also lead to creativity, pre-literacy and pre-numeracy skills, social skills, and problem-solving skills.

Process

1. Gather the children and tell them that they're going to be making a new toy called a Squiggle.
2. Let each kid use a scissors to cut a piece of yarn about 2 feet long. Each piece is a Squiggle.

Free-Range Scissors?

YES. It is okay to allow children to walk away from the activity table with scissors. Real Life involves all kinds of not-sitting-at-a-table scissor scenarios. To prepare for Real Life, kids need opportunities to practice. They learn to manage risk by confronting risk.

We need to trust children to make thoughtful choices around potential hazards. Discuss safety. Remind the children how to hold scissors. Remind them to walk when they are holding scissors. Then let them get to work.

3. Without a word, scatter the Squiggles on the floor.
4. Step back and say something like, "Use your imagination. What can your Squiggle do? What can it become?" Then step offstage and let the children play.
5. Be ready to support their play.

More Play Adventures

- *String of bubbles.* You'll need some *sticky* bubble solution. You can buy it, or you can make your own by combining 2 cups of regular bubble solution, 1 1/2 cups of water, 4 tablespoons of dishwashing liquid, and 4 tablespoons of light corn syrup. Let each child cut a Squiggle about 12 inches long. To play, have the kids scatter the Squiggles on the floor and begin blowing bubbles. One thing will lead to another, and eventually the children will begin playing with their Squiggles. As play progresses, they will realize they can catch bubbles on their Squiggles. The kids will begin doing things like counting the bubbles and discussing the speed and the height and the size of the bubbles. Be ready for a lot of excited squeals and abundant conversation.

- *Create some constructive conflict.* Cut fewer Squiggles than there are children so the kids are forced to share or to come up with other solutions. Not-enough-Squiggles offers them a chance to practice social skills and problem-solving skills. Let the children handle this situation. A lot of times, adults work super hard to eliminate conflict, but what that does is take away children's opportunities to practice handling it.

- *Spiderweb.* This activity involves long Squiggles. Provide several balls of yarn in several different colors and some masking tape. Then challenge the kids to create a spiderweb throughout the room. After the spider web has been created, let them engage in some spiderweb dramatic play. When they are done with it, provide some scissors and let them cut the web apart.

- *Messier Bits o' Fun.* What to do with the little bits of yarn left over after the spiderweb has been cut up? Add them to three or four batches of playdough for some sensory fun. Add them to a mixture of glue and shaving cream or flour and baby oil. Hang contact paper on a wall, stickyside out (attach it using adhesive putty), and stick them to it. Add the pieces to water play or to the sandbox. Blow them around, or suck them up with your vacuum (see chapter 16 on page 66 for more vacuum play ideas).

- *Clothesline.* Let the kids string up some clotheslines with some long Squiggles. Provide clothespins and some *somethings* to hang—socks and washcloths will work well. If some dramatic play starts up, let it flow. Combine this activity with

Going Fishing at Denita's

"Nita! Look! I'm going fishing!" Avery shouted as she cast her squiggle like a fishing line.

That one moment changed the day's Squiggle play. Suddenly, everyone was going fishing. Avery laid her Squiggle down on the floor in a haphazard circle to make a pond, and Jack cast his fishing rod into it. Not content with catching nothing, the children started hooking their Squiggles to buckets that became fish. As play progressed, the Squiggle fishing line and the bucket fish transformed. They became wagons to pull, then dogs on leashes, then sleds to pull up hills, then county fair rides. One imaginary thing led to another and the whole morning slipped away: two hours of imaginative play motivated by some simple Squiggles.

the spiderweb suggestion in the previous variation, and there's a good chance the *somethings* will become bugs caught in the spider's web.

- *Big Squiggles.* Instead of yarn, make squiggles out of 3/8-inch cotton rope. Make a variety of lengths ranging from inchworm to jump rope. Let the children know that these Big Squiggles do not go around their necks, supervise them well, and let them play.

Related Books and Songs

- *The Squiggle* by Carole Lexa Schaefer
- *Lines That Wiggle* by Candace Whitman
- *When a Line Bends . . . A Shape Begins* by Rhonda Gowler Greene
- *Tommaso and the Missing Line* by Matteo Pericoli
- *Line* by Heather Whitely
- "I Walk the Line" by Johnny Cash
- "Conga" by Kids Line Dance Party
- "Electric Slide" by Kids Line Dance Party

Notes

_____

_____

_____

_____

_____

_____

_____

Choose your next adventure: see the next page for a bubble stupendous, or go to page 11 for sensory play that's tremendous.

Bubble House

E ver want to walk inside a giant bubble and do a dance, take a nap, sing a song, or paint a picture? Here's how you can. Oh, and the building process and all the play that follows will help kids learn social skills as well as how to follow directions, take turns, problem solve, and much more.

Process

1. Unroll the plastic and tape the two long ends together.
2. Bunch up one open end of the plastic and securely tape it shut.
3. One the other end, position the fan so it will blow into the bubble and tape the plastic around the fan. Bunch up the remaining plastic and tape it to the side of the fan.

4. Place weights in the milk crate and secure it to the fan.
5. Turn on the fan.
6. Cut a vertical slit about 4 feet long at the opposite end from the fan. This will be the door. Use duct tape to reinforce its perimeter.

More Play Adventures

- *Do stuff in your bubble.* Try things like blowing bubbles, shaping playdough, building with blocks, reading books, eating snacks, or taking naps. How about fingerpainting on the walls? How about dancing or drumming (see chapter 14, page 58)? How about water play? *Everything* is fresh, exciting, and new in the bubble.
- *Use black plastic.* Your bubble experience is different when you can't see through the plastic. And a black bubble house would be a great place for glow-stick play (see chapter 6, page 26).
- *Build your bubble outside instead of inside.* You'll want to add some weight to each corner as you inflate the bubble because even the gentlest wind will upset it. Dumbbells, bricks, and stones work well.

- *Water play.* If you build your bubble outside, why not put a sprinkler inside it for some awesome water play? (You may need to make a few drainage slits in the floor.)
- *Go big.* If you have lots of space, build a bigger bubble. You may need a bigger fan (or more fans), but bigger is always fun. The largest bubble house Jeff has built was 50 feet long, 25 feet wide, and 10 feet tall.

And because this is a complicated project with lots of steps, here are some Bubble House tips, just in case you need them:

- Breathe. If you get frustrated building your bubble house, take a few deep breaths.
- Trust in the tape. If you cut the door too large, you can make it smaller with tape. If the plastic rips during play, you can patch it with tape. If a tape seam splits, you can reinforce it with more tape.
- If it's not windy but your bubble house wants to fly away, either set the fan to a lower speed or make the door a bit larger.
- If it's windy and your bubble house wants to fly away, add some weight to each corner of its floor.

Related Books and Songs

- *Engineering the ABC's: How Engineers Shape Our World* by Patty O'Brien Novak
- *Engineering the City: How Infrastructure Works: Projects and Principles for Beginners* by Matthys Levy and Richard Panchyk
- *Building a House* by Byron Barton
- *Bubble Trouble* by Joy N. Hulme
- *Benny's Big Bubble* by Jane O'Connor
- *Bubble Trouble* by Margaret Mahy
- "Bubbles" by Parachute Express
- "Bubble Ride" by Vanessa Trien and the Jumping Monkeys

Notes

_____

_____

_____

_____

_____

_____

_____

Choose your next adventure: see the next page and they get to pound, or go to page 58 and make some sound.

Ice, Ice Baby

The physical change that occurs when you freeze water never fails to amaze young children. Hammering while wearing goggles never fails to enthrall young children. And searching for hard-to-reach treasure never fails to engage young children. Put all this excitement together, and you have a fantastic learning opportunity loaded with vocabulary, motor skills, cause and effect, trial and error, problem solving, and much, much more.

Process

1. Place various treasures inside the balloons: maybe a single toy dinosaur or a bunch of plastic coins or a handful of glitter. Fill the balloons with water, tie them off, and place them in the freezer.

2. After the water in the balloons is frozen solid, turn the balloons over to the children and let them start exploring. Ask them to predict what will happen when they break

the balloons away from the ice. Then allow them to use scissors to remove the balloons from the ice.

3. After the children have had a chance to explore the giant balloon-shaped ice cubes, have them put on goggles. Place the giant ice cubes on folded towels to help keep them steady, and let the children hammer away—one child-with-a-giant-ice-cube-and-a-hammer at a time. This becomes a good opportunity for the children to practice taking turns and being patient while they wait to hammer away and free the treasures.

Ingredients

- ❑ Balloons
- ❑ Semi-durable treasures small enough to fit in a balloon
- ❑ Water
- ❑ Hammers
- ❑ Goggles
- ❑ Towels

More Play Adventures

- *Add some color.* Add a few drops of liquid watercolor or food coloring to the water balloons before freezing them to create colored ice balloons.

- *Make them stick.* Add a few too-big-to-choke-on magnets to the water balloons before freezing them to create magnetic ice balloons.

- *Mold choices.* You don't have to use balloons! Use something else to mold the ice. You can make one great big sheet of ice with small treasures in it by using a cake pan or a jellyroll pan, or you can use smaller containers like plastic storage containers or cups.

- *Semi-frozen.* Play with your ice balloons *before* they're totally frozen. Typically, you end up with an icy outer shell and an ice-cold inner core—which can be a big surprise for a child with a hammer.

- *Melt ice.* Replace the hammers with warm water and pipettes or turkey basters to melt the ice sheet in order to free the treasures! You can also try using salt, ice melt, or sand to encourage melting.

- *Painting ice.* Start with three large bins of ice cubes. Then make colored water with the children, put out paintbrushes, and let them paint

the ice with the colored water.

- *Icy roads.* Dump a bag or two of ice outside on the driveway or sidewalk on a warm summer day and let the children drive bikes, trikes, and other riding toys across an icy terrain. This can be a challenge and is fun to watch.

- *Sandy ice.* Add a bag or two of ice cubes to your sandbox on a hot summer day. You can even use the hammers and goggles and let those who love hammering hammer away at the smaller pieces of ice in the sand.

- *Color-mixing ice.* Make a bunch of colored ice using liquid watercolors. Place the colored ice in a large tub of cold water, and watch the excitement as the ice melts and colors change. Add some cups, turkey basters, and strainers for pouring, squirting, and dumping fun.

- *Frozen bottles.* This activity is similar to the color-mixing ice play adventure. Put colored water in 20-ounce plastic water bottles and freeze. The kids will have fun pouring out the colored water as the ice slowly melts. Encourage them to come up with ways to speed up the melting process in the bottles.

Related Books and Songs

- *Angelina Ice Skates* by Katharine Holabird
- *Icebergs and Glaciers* by Seymour Simon
- *Smash It! Crash It! Launch It!: 50 Mind-Blowing, Eye-Popping Science Experiments* by Rain Newcomb and Bobby Mercer
- *The Icicle* by Valery Voskoboinikov
- *Icicle Hands and Icicle Knees* by Cindy O'Neil
- "Frozen Face" by Chambers Stevens
- "Frozen" by Alan Patterson

Notes

_____

_____

_____

_____

_____

_____

_____

_____

Choose your next adventure: see the next page for a rain stick that's not, or go to page 145 if your kids like cardboard tubes a lot.

Not a
Rain Stick

Our early learning buddy Claudia Rodriguez in Clarksville, Tennessee, wanted us to come up with plans for a DIY rain stick. While this design is a bit unorthodox, it gets the job done and is a lot easier to make than a traditional-looking rain stick. This activity helps develop listening skills, social skills, and kinesthetic awareness, among other skills.

Process

1. Cut the drainage pipe in half, making two 4-foot pieces. Set one piece aside.
2. Add rice to the first piece of drainage pipe. There is no *right* amount. The sound the Not a Rain Stick makes depends on how much rice you add—and how much you add is up to you. You can add just a little bit and then move the pipe back and forth to get an idea of what the finished product will sound like. When you like the sound you're hearing, you know you've added enough!
3. Align the ends of the rice-filled piece of pipe to create a loop, and duct-tape the two ends together. This is a bit awkward, but it's pretty easy. If you're having trouble, enlist a set of extra hands to get the taping done.
4. Repeat the second and third steps with the second piece of pipe.
5. Shake, roll, turn, toss, and rattle your new Not a Rain Sticks.

More Play Adventures

- *Try different sound-making materials.* Dried beans, dried peas, dried pasta, pebbles, stones, sand, plastic pellets, marbles, golf balls, golf tees, washers, toothpicks—you get the idea. Using different materials—or combinations of materials—will create different sounds.
- *Vary the length of the pipe.* You can make a giant Not a Rain Stick using the whole 8-foot piece of pipe—or maybe a 12-foot piece? Or you can go the other way and make them smaller—cut your pipe into three or four pieces instead of two. The different lengths of pipe will make different sounds, and the kids will interact with them differently.
- *Make matching pairs.* Start out with two 8-foot lengths of pipe and cut each of

them into four equal parts. Create matching pairs of Not a Rain Sticks by including the same sound-making material in each set of two. When the four pairs are finished, toss them all together and let the kids sort them to find the ones with matching sounds.

Related Books and Songs

- *We Shake in a Quake* by Hannah Gelman Givon
- *Never Shake a Rattlesnake* by Michaela Morgan
- *The Rainstick: A Fable* by Sandra Chisholm Robinson
- "Shake, Rattle and Roll" by Bill Haley and His Comets
- "All Shook Up" by Elvis Presley
- "Shake, Rattle and Roll" by Big Joe Turner

Notes

_____

_____

_____

_____

_____

_____

_____

Choose your next adventure: turn the page for some fizzing fun, or go to page 153 for an activity without any sun.

Shake 'n Fizzing
Foamy Fun

Kids love instigating and observing the chemical reaction between baking soda and vinegar. This chapter outlines some of our favorite baking soda and vinegar adventures and offers lots of science and pre-numeracy learning, as well as opportunities to practice social skills.

Process

1. Pour vinegar into the spray bottles and add color.
2. Fill the salt and pepper shakers with baking soda.
3. Place the hand-washing bucket nearby so it's accessible.
4. Step back and let the kids lead the exploration. Be available to assist and support as needed.

Ingredients

- ❑ Baking soda—lots
- ❑ Vinegar—lots
- ❑ Salt and pepper shakers
- ❑ Liquid watercolor
- ❑ Spray bottles
- ❑ Hand-washing bucket

More Play Adventures

- *Slow the reaction.* Add a bit of dish soap to your bottles of vinegar. The dish soap will slow down the chemical reaction.
- *Stretch your vinegar.* You can add water to your vinegar to stretch it a bit. Diluting the vinegar will have some impact on the way it reacts with the baking soda, but not much (unless you water it down a lot).
- *Rainbow volcano.* Instead of putting it in the shakers, pile the baking soda in the shallow tote. Place cups of colored vinegar by the tote, along with pipettes

Keep Off the Lawn

Avoid doing this activity on your lawn if you like your lawn, because the vinegar will kill it off. Denita learned this through experience—and her husband was not too happy. Jeff, on the other hand, prefers doing this on the lawn because it means less lawn to mow and weed.

and other scooping and stirring supplies. Then step back and be ready to follow the children's lead.

- *Go big.* How about putting the baking soda in a large container and using an inexpensive garden sprayer to apply the vinegar?
- *Make it pop.* Collect some plastic 35mm film canisters. (Film used to be used in cameras to make pictures.) Put a bit of baking soda in a canister, dump in some vinegar, quickly snap on the lid, and wait for the *POP*.
- *Make baking soda rocks.* Add just enough water to baking soda, and you can form it into solid clumps. How about hiding small objects (counting bears, beads, coins) in some baking soda rocks and letting the kids dump vinegar on them to uncover the hidden treasures? Or, instead of dumping the vinegar, how about spraying it on with a spray bottle, or dripping it on with an eye dropper, a turkey baster, or a pipette? (Thanks to Lisa Ditlefsen for the idea.)
- *Straw eruptions.* Put about 1 1/2 inches of baking soda into a tote. Fill some cups with colored vinegar. Using a clear straw, capture some vinegar in the straw and stick the straw (with the vinegar still inside) firmly into the baking soda. Then let go of the top of the straw and wait for the reaction to happen. Exciting!
- *Change it around.* Place bowls of colored vinegar into your shallow tote and let the kids use spoons to add the baking soda.

- *Rising balloon.* Put 2 to 3 inches of watered-down vinegar into a 20-ounce bottle. Pour 3 teaspoons of baking soda into a balloon. Attach the balloon to the top of the bottle so it hangs to the side (like a turkey's wattle). When you're ready for the reaction, just lift the balloon and let the baking soda fall into the vinegar.

Related Books and Songs

- *Janice VanCleave's Chemistry for Every Kid: 101 Easy Experiments That Really Work* by Janice VanCleave
- *The Cartoon Guide to Chemistry* by Larry Gonick and Craig Criddle
- *Secret Science: 25 Science Experiments Your Teacher Doesn't Know About* by Steve Spangler
- "Eruption" by Van Halen
- "It's a Chemical Reaction, That's All, All of You" by Fred Astaire
- "Chain Reaction" by US Army Field Band Jazz Ambassadors

Notes

_____

_____

_____

_____

_____

_____

_____

Choose your next adventure: see the next page for soapy reactions, or go to page 70 for frame-based attractions.

Giant
Sudsy Play

Within forty-five minutes of being introduced to the pool noodles, Ethan, a child in Denita's program, ran up and shouted, "Nita! I wonder if these noodles can make bubbles!"

Denita said, "That is an awesome wonder, Ethan! Let's find out. Tell me what you need me to get for you."

Here's some play (and a chance to practice social skills and have a hands-on science experience) based on Ethan's bubble-blowing wondering.

Process

1. Put about 2 inches of bubble solution in a shallow tote.
2. Cut pool noodles in half to form a pair of shorter noodles. Place them nearby the tote.
3. If children don't start blowing through the noodles to make bubbles themselves, then pick up and blow through a noodle yourself. Hard.

More Play Adventures

- *Chalk it up.* Once you've made some suds, kids can scoop some up, plop them onto chalk drawings, rub the suds around, and make colorful suds. Alternatively, you can set up a number of totes with bubble solution, shred a different color of chalk (with a cheese grater) into each tote, and stir (or blow). At Denita's, the children organized themselves into *suds makers*, *suds transporters*, and *car washers* when they used the colorful suds to clean off the toys.
- *Blow them suds.* Suds are great on a windy day. Toss handfuls into the air and watch them fly. If there's no wind, create your own with a fan.

Ingredients

- ❏ Pool noodles
- ❏ Bubble solution (shampoo mixed with water will work fine, but for a fancier bubble solution, try this:
  - ❏ 2/3 cup dishwashing soap
  - ❏ 1 gallon water (add a few drops of food coloring for more colorful bubbles)
  - ❏ 2–3 tablespoons of glycerin (available in pharmacies or chemical supply houses)

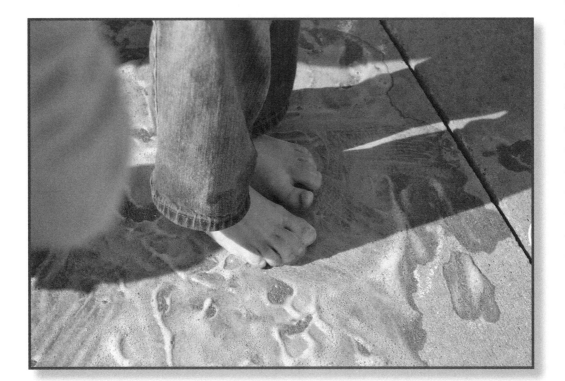

Nurturing I Wonder If's

"I wonder if" moments should be nurtured.

Ethan found that you could use pool noodles to blow bubbles, but it took a tremendous amount of effort and two lungs full of oxygen to find the answer to this wonderful *wonder*. Because one child was given the opportunity to test his wonder, an entire day of sudsy exploration evolved for all of the children in Denita's program. One wonder kept leading right into another.

Too often, kids aren't supported when they *wonder if*. Adults brush the *wonders* aside because the ideas they generate could be time consuming, messy, and inconvenient, especially when they involve topics and materials that aren't part of the day's curriculum.

We believe you should nurture children's *wonders*. Follow up on them. Provide support, offer tools, give time, and make exploration possible.

- *Go small.* Blowing suds in totes with pool noodles is big fun. Now you can go small by using straws to blow bubbles in glasses of chocolate milk. We know this is often considered a no-no, but the fact is, it's a ton of fun. Give it a go.
- *More vacuum fun.* If you happen to have a wet-dry vacuum, dig it out and use it to blow and suck up the suds.
- *More power.* If you happen to have access to an air compressor, you can use it to make lots of suds without all the huffing and puffing. No air compressor? How about a bicycle tire pump?

Related Books and Songs

- *Bubble Bubble* by Mercer Mayer
- *Cinder the Bubble-Blowing Dragon* by Jessica Anderson
- *Fire Bubbles and Exploding Toothpaste: More Unforgettable Experiments That Make Science Fun* by Steve Spangler
- *Pop!: A Book about Bubbles* by Kimberly Brubaker Bradley
- *How to Make Bubbles* by Erika L. Shores
- "I Am a Bubble" by Charlotte Diamond
- "Tiny Bubbles " by Don Ho

Notes

_____

_____

_____

_____

_____

_____

_____

Choose your next adventure: see the next page for painting enlarged, or go to page 20 for playdough recharged.

Big Painting

Painting is typically considered an activity that develops children's small muscles, but if you change up the tools a bit, painting turns into a large-muscle builder that's also big fun! You'll go through more paint, and the mess will get bigger, but big painting is worth the effort.

Process

1. Mix up some paint, one color per tote. You can water it down quite a bit to make it stretch.
2. Add water to another tote for rinsing the giant brushes.
3. Tape large pieces of butcher paper to the large flat surface of your choice.
4. Let the kids dip the brooms and mops into the paint and apply it to the paper.

Ingredients

- ❑ Brooms and mops (use inexpensive ones from a dollar store)
- ❑ Butcher paper
- ❑ Paint—whatever kind you prefer to use
- ❑ Shallow totes
- ❑ Water
- ❑ Large, flat outdoor surface (a driveway, wall, or fence will work)
- ❑ Duct tape

More Play Adventures

- *Mobile painting.* How about duct-taping the mops and brooms to the back of trikes and other ride-on toys so kids can paint while they pedal?
- *Paint with mud.* Paint gets costly. Mix up some soupy mud and use it instead of paint.
- *Paint without paint.* You can paint on concrete surfaces without using paint. Just use water, which will change the color of the surface.

- *Extend their limbs.* How about using tape to attach a large paintbrush to a child's arm or leg? Just tape the end of the brush's handle to the child's limb and let him paint.
- *Not quite as big.* You can use scrub brushes, concrete brushes, large sponges, or paint rollers for big painting that's not quite as big as broom and mop painting.

Related Books and Songs

- *I Ain't Gonna Paint No More!* by Karen Beaumont
- *We'll Paint the Octopus Red* by Stephanie Stuve-Bodeen
- *Mouse Paint* by Ellen Stoll Walsh
- *Purple, Green and Yellow* by Robert Munsch
- *Wait! No Paint!* by Bruce Whatley
- *Elephants Can Paint Too!* by Katya Arnold
- *Color* by Ruth Heller
- *A Color of His Own* by Leo Lionni
- *Colors* by Anne Geddes
- *The Colors of Us* by Karen Katz
- "Black Is the Color" by Stefan Görgner
- "Cicciolina Pink" by Joelle Leandre and Lauren Newton

Notes

_____

_____

_____

_____

_____

_____

_____

_____

Choose your next adventure: see the next page for tubes that are neat, or go to page 160 for a magnet tower that can't be beat.

Awesome Tubes of Fun

These large cardboard tubes are supposed to be used as concrete forms, but we've repurposed them for big play. They are large, but relatively light, so even small kids can easily manipulate them. (Even so, two kids will have to work together to accomplish many of the activities suggested below.) These tubes are a great way to practice social skills, build large-muscle skills, and hone problem-solving skills.

Process

1. Stand the tube on end in the middle of a room.
2. Place a chair next to it. If you want, you can secure the tube to the back of the chair with tape or a bungee cord to keep it stable. We recommend letting the kids be in charge of stabilization.

3. Let the kids take turns dropping stuff into the tube until it is full.
4. Let the kids lift the tube so that all the stuff they filled it with falls out the bottom.
5. Repeat.

More Play Adventures

- *Make smaller tubes.* You can use a utility knife or a handsaw to cut the tube into two sections—one 30 inches long and one 18 inches long. The kids will have fun filling these smaller tubes, and if you leave them around the playroom, the kids will find other uses for them. For example, there is always a use for a cardboard tube in the dramatic play area. We have seen them used as a "cat scan" machine for diagnosing stuffed kitty cats during veterinarian play, as casts for broken arms and legs, and as rolling pins for making pies for nice giants.

- *Make drums.* To create four identical drums, start by slicing an eight- or 12-inch diameter tube into 12-inch sections and then follow the Packing Tape Drum instructions in chapter 14 (page 58). For four slightly different sounding drums, cut the tube into pieces 16, 14, 10, and 8 inches long.

- *Roll them.* Step 1: Lay the tube on its side. Step 2: Roll the tube. You can do this indoors or outdoors. You can do it up a hill or down a hill. You can place things—stuffed animals, balls, pinecones—inside the tube before you roll it, or leave it empty.

- *Build ramps.* Place a tube on its side and elevate one end on the edge of a table or the seat of a chair to create a ramp. Secure it in place with some duct tape or a bungee cord. Let the children slide balls, toy cars, blocks, and other items down the ramp. Alternatively, you can create two C-shaped ramps by carefully slicing a tube in half lengthwise with a utility knife or hand saw. Then let them play.

- *Create tunnels.* With a handsaw, cut an 8- to 12-inch section from a tube. Next, cut the section in half lengthwise to create two arched tunnels. To create more durable tunnels, hot-glue two arches together to create one thicker arch.

- *Construct a giant shake tube.* Start with an 8- or 12-inch diameter tube that is at least 36 inches long. On heavy cardboard, trace around the tube's circumference twice and then cut out the two circles. Use duct tape or packing tape

Ingredients

❑ Cardboard concrete form tube (made by Sakrete, Sonoco, or Quikrete and available at your local home center—usually in a few different diameters)

❑ Chair

❑ Stuff to fill the tube with (try balls, blocks, or wads of newspaper)

to secure one of the circles to an end of the tube. Next, add some items to the tube that will make noise when the kids shake the tube—try golf balls, marbles, washers, bolts, plastic beads, golf tees, toothpicks, or stones. Tape the second cardboard circle to the open end of the tube. Because of the tube's size, the kids will probably have to work together to make noise. You can cut the tube into two smaller sections if you'd prefer to make a couple slightly less gigantic shake tubes.

- *Make blocks.* Start with three or four tubes. Use a hand-saw to cut each tube into uniform sections. You can make eight 6-inch blocks, six 8-inch blocks, or four 12-inch blocks from a 48-inch long tube. These blocks are great for building towers and are pretty durable.
- *Decorate them.* Get creative and embellish your tubes. Try spray paint, tempera paint, glitter paint, latex paint, or acrylic paint. Try stickering, stenciling, glittering, or stamping. Use markers, crayons, colored pencils, or contact paper.

Related Books and Songs

- *Chris Gets Ear Tubes* by Betty Pace
- *Look What You Can Make with Tubes: Creative Crafts from Everyday Objects* edited by Margie Hayes Richmond
- "She's A Beauty" by the Tubes
- "Tube Sox" by Princess Katie & Racer Steve

Notes

Choose your next adventure: see the next page and head for the gutter, or go to page 48 for a project that requires a pipe cutter.

Rain, Rain, Out of the Way

Looking for a versatile and affordable new toy? How about a 10-foot-long plastic rain gutter? They usually cost less than six dollars, so why not get a couple? These babies are loaded with open-ended play potential and all the social, emotional, physical, and cognitive learning that come along for the ride.

Process

1. Use tape to attach one end of the plastic rain gutter to a chair or table.
2. Attach the other end to the floor.
3. Let the kids roll cars or balls down the ramp.

Ingredients

- ❏ 10-foot plastic rain gutter
- ❏ Duct tape
- ❏ Small toy cars and/or balls

- *Double up.* Pair two (or more) lengths of plastic rain gutter to create side-by-side ramps where the kids can race their cars or balls.

- *Water slide.* Head outside and set up a section of rain gutter. Then set up a hose so that it sprays water down the length of the gutter, forming a water slide. (You can secure the hose to the rain gutter with a piece of duct tape.) Let the kids send things down the slide—leaves, pinecones, sticks, hunks of pool noodles, ping-pong balls, ball pit balls, pieces of paper, and so on.

- *More water play.* Set up a series of angled gutter sections so that one spills into the next to create a long water ride for floating toys. Have lots of buckets available to haul and catch water. Use bricks (see chapter 22, page 91 for more brick play ideas) to support the gutter sections. Once they have the ride built, let the children float items on the flowing water. Figuring out the proper way to arrange the gutters and other materials is great trial-and-error learning and a valuable lesson in persistence.

- *Magnet play.* Set up a section of rain gutter so it's suspended between two chairs parallel to the floor. Place some ferrous materials (that is, materials containing iron, such as paperclips, washers, metal ball bearings, and the like) in the gutter, and let the kids use magnet wands to manipulate the materials from below. Alternatively, you can place the magnet wands in the gutter and then hang the ferrous material from below.

- *Get messy.* You can add mess to any of the above ideas by glopping some paint, squirting some liquid water color, dumping some sand, or splatting some mud into the gutter sections.

- *Practice conserving water.* Instead of providing a hose and all the free-flowing water the children want, try limiting the water supply. Fill a large container with water, and explain to the children this is all the water they get to play with. Let them know that they must *conserve*, *recycle*, and *reuse* it, because when the water is gone, the water play is over.

Help them figure out how to use buckets and other containers to catch the water and then send it down the gutter sections again.

- *Create up ramps.* Put a long section of gutter on a slope to create a ramp, and then use your Awesome Vacuum of Play (chapter 16, page 66) to blow balls and other toys up the ramp. This is also fun to do on a flat surface—the vacuum will blast cars and other toys through the gutter. (*Note:* Add a few squiggles of hot glue to the ends of your gutter sections. They will help prevent slippage when kids are building ramps.)
- *Make tunnels.* Cut some 4- to 8-inch long sections of gutter and turn them upside down to create tunnels for toy cars.
- *More ramp ideas.* Try making ramps out of aluminum foil, blankets, plastic sheeting, butcher paper, paper towels, sheets of cardboard, hunks of plywood, and anything else the kids can think of. Experiment a bit and see what works and what doesn't.

Related Books and Songs

- *The River* by Nik Pollard
- *Three Days on a River in a Red Canoe* by Vera B. Williams
- *River* by Judith Heide Gilliland
- *Starry River of the Sky* by Grace Lin
- *Water* by Frank Asch
- *Water, Water Everywhere* by Cynthia Overbeck Bix and Mark J. Rauzon
- *A Drop of Water: A Book of Science and Wonder* by Walter Wick
- "Proud Mary" by Ike & Tina Turner
- "River of Dreams" by Billy Joel

_____

_____

_____

_____

_____

_____

_____

_____

Choose your next adventure: see the next page if you have a bright location, or go to page 95 for exploring saturation.

Shadow Play

Observing shadows is practice for reading because viewing them requires the observer to differentiate between positive and negative space. There are many ways for children to explore shadows, and there is lots of learning potential hidden in the world of shadow play: geometry, spatial relations, identifying patterns, visualizing positive and negative space, and more.

Process

1. Make your room as dark as possible so that you can control the shadows. Turn off the overhead lights and draw blinds, close curtains, or hang thick blankets over windows.

2. If you don't have an empty section of wall, hang a flat white bed sheet. You can tape it to a wall or drape it over a table or chair to create a smooth surface you can project shadows onto.

Ingredients

❏ A light source other than the overhead lighting (flashlights, table lamps, and lanterns work great)
❏ Duct tape
❏ Blank wall or flat white bed sheet

Don't Burn Your House Down

A morning of shadow-making fun will come to a quick end if your house catches on fire. Take a few simple steps to keep things safe:

- Avoid light sources using incandescent and halogen bulbs. These bulbs get hot, and if they come in contact with a flammable surface—or a child's skin—things could get ugly. Opt for fluorescent or LED bulbs instead because they produce less heat.
- Tape that cord. If you need to use an extension cord to get your lighting where it needs to be, make sure you tape the cord to the floor so it's less of a tripping hazard.
- Talk about safety. Take a moment to talk to the kids about safety around cords and light fixtures. You don't need to make it into a big lecture; just remind them to be careful.

3. Turn on your shadow-generating light source and arrange it so that it shines on the smooth surface.
4. Position yourself between the light and the wall or sheet, and then demonstrate how to make shadows.
5. Let the kids take over and create their own shadow play experience.

More Play Adventures

- *Name that shadow.* Hang a sheet in the middle of the room. Put the light source a few feet behind the sheet and 3 to 6 feet off the floor. Ask one child to stand between the light source and the sheet and the rest of the children to stand on the other side of the sheet. Ask the lone child to hold up a mystery object and let the rest of the children try to guess what the object is, based on its shadow.

- *Who is it?* Using the same setup as in the previous play adventure, have the children sit down on one side of the sheet and cover their eyes. Quietly

lead one child from the group to the other side of the sheet. Then tell the group to open their eyes and guess whose body is making the shadow.

- *Great big monster shadows.* With the same basic setup, place the light source as close to the floor as possible. This changes the perspective of the shadows. They will be *huge.* To really make your monster scary, use multiple light sources—four or five flashlights, for example, instead of one. Now let the kids take turns making monster shadows for one another. You can provide a supply of materials like pipe cleaners, hats, capes, and hoops—whatever you have for the children to hold and wear to enhance their monster shadows.

- *Silly sculpture shadows.* Set things up like the first variation—light source, about 2 feet of space, a sheet, and an audience on the other side—but this time have a table behind the sheet and set the light source on the table. Let kids use random materials (for example, pipe cleaners, boxes, construction paper, rocks) and tape to build silly sculptures and place them between the light source and the sheet. They can go to the audience side of the sheet to check out the shadow their creation casts.

- *Flashlight shadows.* Give each child a flashlight or two and let the shadow-making fun begin. When the children each have their own flashlight, all the control is in their hands. They control the light sources, the perspective, and all the shadow fun.

- *Witness wild shadows.* Each day make an effort to point out shadows in your house and in your yard. Encourage the children to pay attention to how the shadows of the trees move during the day and to notice how at certain times the shadows are very long and at other times they are almost nonexistent.

- *Fill in shadows.* Outside, use loose parts to fill in the shadows cast by trees, play structures, and other objects.
- *Other light play.* Instead of shadows, create some play by focusing light with magnifying glasses or refracting light with prisms and crystals.

Related Books and Songs

- *Whoo's There? A Bedtime Shadow Book* by Heather Zschock
- *The Art of Hand Shadows* by Albert Almoznino
- *Hand Shadows and More Hand Shadows* by Henry Bursill
- *Me and My Shadows: Shadow Puppet Fun for Kids of All Ages* by Elizabeth Adams and Bud Banis
- *The Little Book of Hand Shadows* by Phila H. Webb and Jane Corby
- *Shadow* by Suzy Lee
- *Shadows and Reflections* by Tana Hoban
- *The Dark, Dark Night* by M. Christina Butler
- "Shadow Dancing" by Andy Gibb
- "Sillouettes" by the Diamonds
- "Me and My Shadow" by Frank Sinatra

Notes

_____

_____

_____

_____

_____

_____

_____

Choose your next adventure: see the next page and make blocks with books, or go to page 141 and take a look.

Book Blocks

Have a closet full of romance novels no one wants and you'll never read again? Or a stack of old textbooks taking up space? What about the pile of phone books delivered to your house every year? (Who still uses phone books?) We've got a way to put those space-takers to work: Make them into blocks that will inspire social, physical, emotional, and cognitive learning. It's simple to do, they'll freshen up your block play area, and you'll get a bit of space back in that storage closet you've been meaning to clean out.

Process

1. Carefully wrap each book in duct tape.
2. Add your new blocks to your block play area.

More Play Adventures

- *Make patterns.* Use multiple colors of duct tape and let the kids create patterns on the blocks—checkers, diagonal lines, zigzags, stripes.
- *Skip the tape.* Let the kids use contact paper instead of duct tape to wrap the book blocks. This provides a wide variety of patterns to try.
- *Personalize them.* Allow kids to cut pieces of cardstock the size of the book covers, draw on them, and then attach them to the front and back of each book before covering it with clear box tape. They can also make blocks with words, letters, numbers, and shapes on them this way.
- *Go big.* Let the kids build bigger blocks by sandwiching two, three, or more books of the same size together.

Related Books and Songs

- *Changes, Changes* by Pat Hutchins
- *Block City* by Robert Louis Stevenson
- *Building a House* by Byron Barton
- *Iggy Peck, Architect* by Andrea Beaty
- *Block Building for Children: Making Buildings of the World with the Ultimate Construction Toy* by Lester Walker and Witold Rybczynski
- "We Built This City" by Starship
- "It's Time to Read" by Mar Harman
- "Read to Me" by Music with Mar

Ingredients

- ❑ Old books (Paperbacks work best—mass markets, phone books, textbooks)
- ❑ Duct tape (gray is fine, but colors are better)

_____

_____

_____

_____

_____

_____

_____

Choose your next adventure: turn the page for magnetic action, or go to page 30 for block making action.

Magnet Play Tower

The Magnet Play Tower is a very simple-to-build project that creates a dedicated place for magnet play. All you need to build it is a few tin cans, some colored duct tape, and magnets. This sort of magnet play is full of exploratory learning that, among other things, builds understanding of the physical world, problem-solving skills, and cause-and-effect thinking. Keep in mind that small magnets can potentially be a choking hazard. Also remember that with thoughtful supervision, magnets can be perfectly safe.

Process

1. Make sure your cans are clean and free of sharp edges.
2. Stack one can on top of another and duct tape them together.
3. Set the third can on top of the two you just taped together and secure it to them with duct tape.
4. Use more duct tape to decorate your new Magnet Play Tower.
5. Get out the magnets and let kids discover the way they stick to the Magnet Play Tower.

Ingredients

❑ Three or more #10 cans (The big ones—they hold 96 fluid ounces. Any #10 can will work, but we're partial to #10 cans of pudding, nacho sauce, and chocolate syrup because those things are super-yummy.)
❑ Duct tape—assorted colors
❑ Scissors
❑ Magnets—assorted

More Play Adventures

- *Attach it.* Provide kids with materials like pipe cleaners, feathers, bits of fabric, and scraps of construction paper, and then get out of their way and let them figure out how they can attach the materials to the tower using the magnets.
- *Fabulously ferrous.* Provide metallic bits— like paper clips, finish nails, or metal jar lids—for your magnets to pick up.
- *Sideways.* Lay your Magnet Play Tower on its side on the floor to create a rolling magnet play experience. We've seen kids scatter pieces of magnetic hematite across the floor and then use a Magnet Play Tower as a "rolling vacuum thingy" to collect the pieces. "They just snap on when I roll it by!" was how an excited three-year-old girl explained it.
- *Hang the tower.* Hang your Magnet Play Tower. Before taping on the top can, carefully drill or punch a hole in its top, thread through a piece of nylon twine, and secure the twine on the inside of the can so it doesn't pull through the hole. Then tape the can to the others and hang your tower

from a hook in the ceiling or from a tree branch. The Magnet Play Tower will sway when kids stick the magnets to it.

- *Go big.* Use more #10 cans to build more towers, taller towers, double-wide towers, and odd-shaped towers. If you build a tower more than three cans tall, place some weight in the bottom can (a few stones, or a brick or two) to help keep your tower from toppling over.
- *Go small.* You can, of course, deconstruct the tower and provide the kids with single cans to use as personal magnet play stations, or you can use smaller, soup can–sized cans to create mini magnet towers.

Related Books and Songs

- *What Makes a Magnet?* by Franklyn M. Branley
- *Forces Make Things Move* by Kimberly Brubaker Bradley
- *What Magnets Can Do* by Allan Fowler
- *Magnets* by Anne Schreiber
- *Magnets: Pulling Together, Pushing Apart* by Natalie M. Rosinsky
- *Amazing Magnetism* by Rebecca Carmi
- "Just Stick It" by Denita Dinger (sung to the tune of "Beat It" by Michael Jackson, with the following lyrics)

    We have some magnets and a tower of cans
    Stick them on there, just use your hands
    Not quite sure just how it works
    Let's go to Google and do a search
    Just stick it . . . Just stick it . . .

- "Stuck on You" by Elvis Presley
- "Stuck Like Glue" by Sugarland
- "Opposites Attract" by Bill Nye
- "Sticky Bubble Gum" by Carole Peterson

Notes

_____

_____

_____

_____

_____

_____

_____

_____

Choose your next adventure: turn the page and the book's pretty much done, or go to page 87 for a bit more fun.

Learning Term Glossary

Language Skills

Conversation skills: Conversation skills make up the ability to engage in conversation with another person. This requires other skills, such as the ability to listen, read body language, make eye contact, and take turns.

Letter recognition: This is the ability to recognize certain squiggles called *letters* that have names like *A*, *H*, and *Q* and that represent sounds like *ahh*, *huh*, and *quh*.

Storytelling: This is the ability to convey information through words and sounds. Some storytelling involves magic unicorns and fairies, and other storytelling involves what happened at breakfast or plans for the afternoon.

Understanding/following directions: This is the ability to complete tasks based on instructions. Younger kids can follow very simple instructions like "Get the red ball," and older kids can follow more complex multistep instructions like "After you finish your snack, go to the toy box, get the big red ball, and bring it to me."

Vocabulary: A child's vocabulary is the body of words the child "owns"—the words he can say, identify in print, use in conversation, and know the meaning of.

Word meaning: This means understanding the specific meanings of individual words based on personal experiences involving the ideas behind the words. *Grandma*, *kitten*, and *ice cream* have different meanings based on the experience of the people using the words. For example, *kitten* means something different to a child who has a real kitten at home than it does to a child who has only seen kittens in pictures.

Word recognition: This is the knowledge that certain sets of squiggles called *words* have special meanings that other sets of squiggles do not. Word recognition is the ability to tell which squiggles are which—the ability to identify that *dad* is a word and that @#$* is not.

Number Skills

Algebraic thinking: Algebraic thinking may seem too complicated for young children, but the foundations for this formalized way of processing information are laid in childhood. Algebraic thinking includes seeing patterns, noticing mathematical situations, identifying quantitative relationships, and perceiving change. Each of these is defined below.

Noticing mathematical situations: Mathematical situations are basically all the number-related events children encounter ("She has more chips than I do!", "Look, we have the same shirts today! That means two Batman shirts," "That cat has two eyes, just like me!"). Learning to recognize these math-related events helps children value the power of numbers and logical thinking and also prepares them for later learning.

Identifying quantitative relationships: This means seeing relationships that have to do with quantity. ("Reggie has six carrot sticks. Does anyone have more than that? Who has the fewest carrot sticks?") It means giving attention to the amount of *this* or the number of *that*.

Perceiving change: This means paying attention to changes over time. ("Look at how the oak tree has changed again. In the winter, all the leaves were gone, but then they came back in the spring, got big in the summer, and are turning colors and falling off now.")

Data analysis: This is the ability to skim useful knowledge from pools of information. For example, children who track what happens when they dump a variety of liquids into bowls of baking soda may make the useful discovery that the baking soda makes bubbles whenever vinegar is added.

Estimation: An estimation is an educated guess about the worth, size, quantity, or range of something. As children have more experiences, their ability to estimate increases.

Geometric thinking: This kind of thinking involves lines, shapes, and space. Children engage in geometric thinking when they draw triangles, stack blocks into cardboard boxes, and line up Hot Wheels cars on the floor.

Measurement: Measurement is the act of determining the size, quantity, length, or amount of something. Kids do this when they help bake cookies, when they count the blocks in a tower, and when they stand back-to-back with a friend to see who is taller.

Number recognition: This is the ability to recognize certain special squiggles (and combinations of squiggles) called *numbers* that have names like *one*, *forty-three*, and *seven thousand two hundred ten*.

One-to-one correspondence: This is the ability to match items from one set with items from a second set. Children do this when they match napkins with plates while setting the table, when they match hands with mittens when going out to play in the snow, and when they match arriving parents to kids at the end of the day.

Seeing patterns: Patterns are reliable traits, acts, tendencies, and other observable characteristics of people and things. Young children devote a lot of time to seeing patterns. Through observation they learn that the sun *always* comes up in the east and goes down over there in the west and that it *always* gets dark after the sun goes down. They learn that dropped toys *always* fall down and *never* fall up. They learn that in child care they *always* wash their hands before they eat.

Personal Skills

Initiative: This is the ability to independently act, decide, or take charge of situations. Children show initiative when they go to the bathroom on their own, when they choose an activity, and when they decide to make their own breakfast.

Self-awareness: This is a person's knowledge of her individual traits, values, personality, feelings, behaviors, and other characteristics. Children become self-aware over time as they discover that they are individuals who exist as part of a group ("Claire and me are both girls, but she has green eyes, and my eyes are brown," "I do not want to eat those carrots," "I love to climb on stuff").

Self-confidence: This is a person's belief in himself and his personal skills, abilities, and resources. Self-confidence is a self-assured freedom from doubt ("I can dress myself," "I'm the best jumper ever!" "Sam can't catch me when we play tag").

Self-help skills: These are the basic abilities required to take care of one's own needs—washing hands, wiping nose, using the bathroom independently, brushing teeth, tying, zipping, buttoning, and so on.

Self-regulation: This is an individual's ability to manage her own emotions, behaviors, desires, and actions ("I'm waiting my turn," "I will wait for my mother before crossing the street," "I'm really mad at my brother and want to hit him, but I'm not going to").

Physical Skills

Auditory discernment: This is the ability to distinguish between sounds. For example, being able to distinguish the sound of the letter *P* from the sounds of the letters *B* and *D* or loud sounds from quiet ones.

Hand-eye coordination: This is the ability to coordinate eye movement with hand movement in order to complete tasks. Examples include picking up dropped peas from the floor after serving lunch to a herd of toddlers, popping soap bubbles with fingers on a sunny afternoon, or catching lightning bugs after sunset.

Kinesthetic awareness: This is an understanding of the movement and position of one's body in space. This awareness contributes to a person's ability to maintain balance and move fluidly. Children develop this awareness during play as they tumble, climb, jump, roll, fall, wrestle, and spin.

Large-muscle control: This is the ability to regulate and coordinate movement of the big muscles in the arms, legs, and core. In young children, developing large-muscle control also involves building muscle strength. Children learn this control during active play: running, wrestling, climbing, jumping, hopping, skipping, and so on.

Olfactory discernment: This is the ability to differentiate experiences via the sense of smell. A child does this when he runs into the house after playing in the yard and knows that Grandma has made chocolate chip cookies.

Sensory awareness: This is the ability to collect, discern, and process sensory stimuli. Included here are the five standard senses (sight, touch, hearing, taste, and smell) as well as others that many people are not aware of: proprioception (awareness of where body parts are relative to other body parts), nociception (the brain's system for receiving pain signals), equilibrioception (the brain's way of balancing and sensing body movement in terms of acceleration and directional changes), thirst (the sense system that monitors hydration level), and hunger (the system that monitors when we need to eat).

Small-muscle control: This is the ability to manage small-muscle movement, dexterity, reflexes, grasping pressure, coordination, and synchronization. Children develop these skills as they pick up worms during outside play, pound mounds of playdough, and dig boogers from their noses.

Tactile discernment: This is the ability to differentiate experiences using the sense of touch. Children develop this ability through hands-on interaction with the world as they manipulate and connect with different materials. Over time, they learn that their favorite stuffed animal is *soft*, the concrete sidewalk is *hard*, the water in the tub is *wet*, and the stove is *hot*.

Taste discernment: This is the ability to differentiate between experiences using the sense of taste. It's developed through mouth-on interaction with the world. With practice, children learn the differences between strawberries, broccoli, chocolate cake, pinecones, fries, mud, and lemonade.

Visual discernment: This is the ability to differentiate between experiences using vision. It's developed through eyes-on interaction with the world. Over time, children learn to tell the difference between *red* and *blue*, *near* and *far*, *bright* and *dim*, *foreground* and *background*.

Social Skills

Adaptability: This is the ability to go with the flow—to change or be changed to fit current circumstances. Children learn adaptability when rain delays a much anticipated field trip, when they end up with the blue cup instead of the green one at lunch, or when a best friend does not show up to play.

Collaboration: This is the ability to work with one or more persons to complete a task. The ability to collaborate requires other social skills, such as nonverbal communication, adaptability, and empathy. Children hone collaboration skills when they play team sports, engage in dramatic play, and work on projects in small groups.

Conflict-resolution skills: These are the social, personal, and thinking skills used to resolve disagreements and differences with others. Learning these skills takes time and using them effectively takes practice. Children must also learn which conflict resolution skills are socially acceptable. For example, many toddlers use biting as an effective way to resolve conflicts with peers (You're annoying me . . . CHOMP!), but they eventually learn there are more acceptable ways to deal with such situations (You're annoying me . . . I'm going to go play over there).

Contribution: This is the act of giving to the greater social community. This may mean someone brings treats on her birthday, takes turns, or shows to others the awesome bug she's found, but it also means not throwing a fit, or not biting someone or punching someone when she doesn't get her way.

Empathy: This is the act of understanding or being sensitive to the feelings of others—the ability to see things from another person's perspective. This skill develops over time in most children as they connect with the people around them. They move from a me-centric view of the world to a worldview that takes the feeling of others into account.

Listening skills: Listening skills allow people to hear with understanding. These skills allow children to receive auditory information, attend to it, understand it, and respond to it. Listening skills include things like making eye contact, managing body language, asking questions, showing empathy, and concentrating on what is being said.

Nonverbal communication: This is the process of sending and receiving information through gestures, posture, eye movement, and touch. It is something children practice during dramatic play, outside play, small-group time, meals, and one-on-one time with adult caregivers.

Patience: This is the ability to peacefully accept delay. Children learn this when they take turns, when they must wait a few moments for a glass of water, and when they count down the days until their birthday.

Sense of community: This is a feeling of belonging or inclusion—a feeling of being part of a group. Developing a sense of community takes time—children have to feel comfortable, secure, and emotionally safe before they can feel that they belong.

Thinking Skills

Cause and effect: This is the ability to comprehend relationships between actions and reactions. Plastic keys always fall down when dropped, and Daddy always picks them up; the cat leaves the room if her tail gets pulled too often; ice cream cones make a big mess if you don't eat them quickly.

Creativity: This is the ability to produce or identify options, ideas, alternatives, or possibilities. Children practice creativity when they are free to explore and play with open-ended materials such as sand, water, cardboard boxes, sticks, and clay.

Discernment: This is the act of perceiving, observing, or noticing differences with the mind or senses. Children use this skill to sort, classify, and understand the world. This is why it is important that learning experiences are as sensory-rich as possible—the more our senses are involved, the more we learn.

Drawing conclusions: This is the ability to combine multiple pieces of information to make an inference—a reasoned conclusion. This skill takes practice—young children's conclusions are often outlandishly humorous because they do not have as much information to draw upon as adults do. For example, a rabbit pulled from a hat is real magic to a three-year-old, but it's a neat trick to an eight-year-old who's just read a book about magic tricks.

Inquisitiveness: This is a state of active curiosity—a drive to investigate, research, ask questions, and seek knowledge. We humans are born wired for inquisitiveness—it is an evolutionary strategy that helps hardwire our big brains and prepares us for survival.

Object permanence: This is the understanding that objects continue to exist even when they cannot be seen, heard, or touched. It takes time for this ability to develop. If they can't experience them with their senses, things do not exist for newborns. As they develop, they come to understand that the ball they were playing with still exists after it rolls into the tall grass.

Problem-solving skills: This is the process of working through the particulars of a problem to reach a solution. Children develop this skill as they explore, observe, attempt, fail, and succeed during play. For example, learning to build a stable block tower requires many attempts and failures, lots of observing as other people build towers, and much fumbling before success can be achieved.

Qualitative change: This is change relating to the quality of something (such as its size, appearance, or value) rather than its quantity. Children learn this as they mix different colors of paint together, watch mud pies dry in the sun, and observe tomato plants grow, flower, and fruit.

Symbolic representation: This is the ability to use one object to represent another. Using a block to represent a smartphone during dramatic play leads to using squiggles on paper to represent ideas learned in school.

Jeff A. Johnson worked as a center director and family child care provider for twenty-five years before retiring in the summer of 2013 to pursue his hobbies full time. In his retirement, Jeff writes books, produces podcasts, creates digital content, makes toys, visits early learning programs, advocates for play, defends childhood, and speaks at events in the United States, Canada, and anyplace else that will have him. You can connect with Jeff online at

jeffajohnson@cableone.net
www.explorationsearlylearning.com
www.jeffajohnson.com
www.facebook.com/explorationsearlylearning
www.youtube.com/user/ExplorationsLLC
http://pinterest.com/exearlylearning

Denita Dinger has been a family child care provider since 1998. She spent six years transitioning her family child care/preschool program to a play-based, child-led learning environment. Making the change taught Denita valuable lessons. She loves to share what she's learned with others and since 2009 has been a keynote presenter at a wide variety of early childhood professional events. Denita lives in Sioux Falls, South Dakota, with her husband, Leroy, and children, Myah and Landon. You can connect with Denita at

steelerfan.dd@gmail.com
www.playcounts.com
http://playcountsdenitadinger.blogspot.com
www.facebook.com/pages/Play-Counts/141352815884541

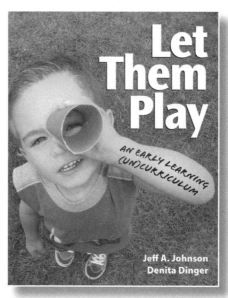